M000080239

Kevin's book brings to the Body of Christ a refreshing and clear look at this particular part of our journey called "the wilderness." Kevin brings insight and revelation that is very much needed for this generation and generations to come. His book, "A Word for the Weary," will help each individual pass through this place victoriously. Kevin speaks to each reader with a prophetic edge and this increases God's personal touch on this teaching. I, personally, have gained insight and wisdom and enjoyed reading his book "A Word for the Weary."

—Gail Manizak

The Power and Presence Ministry

Author: "It's God's Word, not Mine . . ."

Many years ago, I saw a four or five year old little boy in our church Sunday school. As time passed I lost contact with him but a few years ago I was reconnected to him as a young man, a father, with a lovely wife and three children. What I discovered was Kevin had grown into a mighty man of God. Today everyone in our church marvels at his growth and amazing understanding of God's Word. He also now serves as one of our pastors. Not only do I highly endorse his ministry to you, but I believe every reader will greatly benefit from his book, "A Word for the Weary."

—Pastor Donald Riling

Senior Pastor, Brockport Christian Center Church

Director/Chairman, Leadership International

A Word
for the Weary

40 DAYS
OF WALKING THROUGH THE WILDERNESS

KEVIN STEVENS

AMBASSADOR INTERNATIONAL
GREENVILLE, SOUTH CAROLINA & BELFAST, NORTHERN IRELAND

www.ambassador-international.com

A Word for the Weary

40 Days of Walking Through the Wilderness

© 2016 by Kevin Stevens, All rights reserved

ISBN: 978-1-62020-551-8

eISBN: 978-1-62020-473-3

Scripture marked NIV taken from THE HOLY BIBLE, NEW INTERNATIONAL VERSION®, NIV® Copyright © 1973, 1978, 1984, 2011 by Biblica, Inc.® Used by permission. All rights reserved worldwide.

Scripture marked NKJV taken from the New King James Version®. Copyright © 1982 by Thomas Nelson. Used by permission. All rights reserved.

Scripture marked KJV taken from The King James Version, The Authorized Version.

Scripture marked ESV taken from The ESV® Bible (The Holy Bible, English Standard Version®) copyright © 2001 by Crossway, a publishing ministry of Good News Publishers. ESV® All rights reserved.

Scripture marked NLT taken from the Holy Bible, New Living Translation, copyright © 1996, 2004, 2007 by Tyndale House Foundation. Used by permission of Tyndale House Publishers, Inc., Carol Stream, Illinois 60188. All rights reserved.

Scripture quotations taken from the Amplified® Bible, Copyright © 1954, 1958, 1962, 1964, 1965, 1987 by The Lockman Foundation Used by permission. (www.Lockman.org)

Cover Design & Typesetting by Hannah Nichols

Ebook Conversion by Anna Riebe Raats

AMBASSADOR INTERNATIONAL
411 University Ridge, Suite B14
Greenville, SC 29601
www.ambassador-international.com

AMBASSADOR BOOKS
The Mount
2 Woodstock Link
Belfast, BT6 8DD, Northern Ireland, UK
www.ambassadormedia.co.uk

The colophon is a trademark of Ambassador

This book is dedicated to my wife Bridgett for always believing in me even when I didn't, to my three beautiful children Jace, Jeremiah, and Hannah who give me a reason to breathe each and every day, and to Jesus for being such a wonderful God who brings us in and through every season of our lives. Words are not enough Lord to give You the glory You deserve.

FOREWORD

A WORD FOR THE WEARY is a book that I could not put down. While reading it, I lost track of time and what I was currently working on. Written from the heart of God, sharing the life models of men and women, patriarchs and matriarchs of old who lived by faith and not by sight, this book outlines in chronological order the life lessons that we all in one way or another can relate to. It is refreshing to know that we are not alone in our life journey to fulfill the call of God on ones' life. To read these inspiring, encouraging, challenging, uplifting and relatable encounters reassures the reader that God has preordained, predestined and already ordered your steps.

A Word for the Weary is the anthem for believers that the Scripture in Galatians 6:9 declares "And let us not be weary in well doing: for in due season we shall reap, if we faint not" (KJV). This book is beautifully written and well-articulated to reach a broad audience. Kevin Stevens is a prophetic and apostolic leader called to his generation to ignite revival fires, impart the Father's heart, and cause believers to maximize their full potential and call in God. This book will help readers to identify what season they may be currently in, walking out of or entering into. Kevin challenges the reader to overcome personal trials, tribulations, and circumstances that subtly come to rob a person of their identity, calling, and purpose in God. It was written with you in mind. *A Word for the Weary* is a book that will assist you through your own 40-day probation period of your life.

In other words, when you have an understanding of your wilderness places and seasons in God, you come to realize that He will sometimes require you to make sudden transitions. Kevin helps the reader to mark those areas of their lives while assisting them in walking in prophetic fulfillment and relating with the pioneering characters of the Bible that overcame and conquered places that ultimately brought about personal and corporate victory and success for God's leaders and people.

I highly recommend this anointed, inspiring, and empowering literature for all who desire to upgrade in their walk with God and fulfill their God-given calling in their generation. The captivating stories and words written on these pages will enhance, bless, and inspire you with the Issachar anointing to know what season you may be in and know what to do in it. This 40-day devotional will make you stronger by the Spirit when you are feeling weak or weary which I can attest to after reading this remarkable book of real life stories and truths.

—Dr. Hakeem Collins

Founder and President,

Hakeem Collins Ministries, Revolution Network

Author of *Born to Prophesy: God's Voice Speaking Through You*

Wilmington, Delaware

www.hakeemcollinsministries.com

INTRODUCTION

"The Lord God has given Me
The tongue of the learned,
That I should know how to speak
A word in season to him who is weary.
He awakens Me morning by morning,
He awakens My ear
To hear as the learned."

—Isaiah 50:4 NKJV

IN YOUR JOURNEY WITH THE Lord, have you ever found yourself in a season of seemingly wandering through the wilderness? It may be a crushing and difficult situation you find yourself in. Perhaps the trials and turmoil of life have seemed relentless in the pursuit of your peace. Maybe it has been so long since you have experienced and sensed the presence of God in your life. It may even seem you are in a dry desert land where the sun has beaten you down and left your soul parched. There are many circumstances and causes that can leave us feeling like we are held bound in the wilderness. Nevertheless, if you are experiencing this presently, I encourage you to keep reading!

I believe in this very moment the Lord wants to remind you, the reader, that the work He has begun in you He will be faithful to complete. The call of God and the anointing He has placed on your life have never left you. At this present moment you may feel like you are desolate, forsaken, and alone like a ship left out to sea. It may seem as if God is in some far and distant place unaware of your circumstances and the current pain you are experiencing. But the Lord would have you to know that the wilderness place is not unknown to many that have gone before you. And it is most definitely not unknown to Him! As you read through the pages of Scripture it is most evident that every mighty man and woman of God had to go through severe periods of trial, testing, and tribulation in the wilderness. It would seem that God has designed periods in the wilderness to precede usefulness in the kingdom of God. Even Jesus after He was baptized in the Jordan River and the Holy Spirit came down upon Him, the Scriptures tell us that immediately the Spirit of God led Him into the wilderness for forty days and nights.

My dear brothers and sisters, you are not alone in your wilderness place! God is not finished with you! His promises have not left you! His Spirit has not left you nor His calling, plans, and purposes for your life. But rather, through your wilderness place God is both conforming you into the image of His Son, Jesus Christ, and He is preparing you for the high call of God He has placed upon your life. There are no shortcuts to becoming all that God desires for you to be. The Lord knows exactly what you need to reach your full potential in Jesus Christ. God doesn't just see you as you are presently. The Lord sees what you will become through His mighty power working within you! Are you weary? Are you exhausted from the pressures of life? Do you feel trapped in that wilderness place? The word of the Lord to you is this: **"I will open rivers in high places, and fountains in the midst of the valleys: I will make the wilderness a pool of water, and the dry land springs of water" (Isaiah 41:18 KJV).** God will see you through your wilderness and you will find His supernatural strength will empower you in your hour of need. You may not understand what He is doing now, but in time and through your wilderness you will come to know the faithfulness of God like never before. As you read through the pages of this book, may your hearts be encouraged, your lives transformed, and your strength renewed. To God be all the glory.

ABRAM

CALLED OUT

DAY 1

And Terah took Abram his son, and Lot the son of Haran his son's son,
and Sarai his daughter in law, his son Abram's wife; and they went
forth with them from Ur of the Chaldees, to go into the land of
Canaan; and they came unto Haran, and dwelt there.

—Genesis 11:31 KJV

Imagine with me walking in the shoes of Abram. Entrenched all around you are the false gods of the nation around you. Even your father, Terah, has been deeply infected with their idolatrous worship and has joined right in with them. One day, in a moment's notice, your father decides to move your whole family from Ur, everything you once knew, to an unknown land called Haran. Haran could be best described as a desert-like place, most undesirable and definitely not what you had in mind. To add to the situation, once you get settled in Haran, your father, Terah, dies. Life has changed drastically, unexpectedly, and suddenly.

Have you ever felt this way? Have you ever felt the pain of life's inconsistencies? I'm sure you have! Life for Abram was anything but easy for this portion of his life. I know we can probably all relate to Abram on various levels. The word "Haran" is very interesting in its definition. In Hebrew it means *to melt, burn, or literally dry up*. It is very likely that the place Haran, the place of being dried up, could have well-spoken of the condition of Abram's soul at that current time. Although Abram had married Sarai, she was unable to have children at this point. Surely this was most burdensome to them both. It is very possible Abram was in a very dry, tiring, and discouraging place in his life. It seems Abram was in a wilderness place! But little did Abram realize it; the Lord was setting Abram up to reveal Himself to him in a mighty way. The Lord was getting ready to open up the eyes of Abram's understanding.

Did you realize that the Lord has divinely designed those dry periods and wilderness places in our lives to prepare us to receive a greater revelation of Himself? It is those wilderness experiences in our lives that not only grab our attention but also teach us to thirst for the presence of the Lord, to seek His face, and to draw ever closer to Him. If you are in dry and wilderness-type place, get ready because the Lord is getting you ready to experience Him in a fresh, new way!

Look at what happens next. Life is going on for Abram as it was and the Lord reveals Himself to Abram, speaks directly into his life, and gives Abram clear direction to leave Haran along with his father's family to go into a land that He would show Abram. Not only did the Lord give Abram a command, He gave him a most precious promise attached with His instructions that He would bless Abram, make him famous, and that He would turn him into a great nation. But there's only one thing. God did not tell Abram the full details of where he would be going. The Lord just told Abram to go to a land He would show him. Initially to Abram this could have added to his wilderness experience! Not knowing, Abram did obey, but where would he go? How would God bring His promise to pass? Is it too good to be true? Abram was called out by God. God would bless Abram's obedience and He will bless ours when we step out in faith and obedience to His voice in our lives. You have been called out by the Lord. Yes, you may feel like you are in Haran, a dry desert place, but the Lord is getting ready to do some great things in your life. You watch, you wait, you'll see.

ABRAM

TIME OF TRANSITION

DAY 2

Now the LORD had said to Abram:
"Get out of your country,
From your family
And from your father's house,
To a land that I will show you."

—Genesis 12:1 NKJV

Times of transition can be some of the most difficult and challenging seasons in our lives. We as people become so accustomed to doing things the same way and getting comfortable in the same routines, but God has a way of almost always interrupting our little plans in order to bring about His marvelous purposes in our lives. But it doesn't come without the much-needed transitions to bring us from point A to point B and so on. Oftentimes, the Lord will take us spiritually speaking up to the mountaintop. Off in the far distance the Lord will enable us to see something that He will fulfill and bring to pass in our lives. But what God does not share with us is how we will reach the fulfillment of His promise. As we look from the mountaintop to the valley below all we can see are the dark clouds that loom heavily above. We know we must pass through that valley place to get to the place the Lord has promised us. Slowly we start to descend off of the mountaintop and enter into the valley place and into TRANSITION.

Here Abram had been given a glorious promise by God, but he had no idea what he would encounter in the days ahead in accordance with that promise. Leaving Ur, moving into Haran, and then being called out by God to go to some unknown land. I want to encourage you with this word from the Lord. Transitions are a *normal* and a *necessary* part of not only growth but getting to the divine destination God has intended for your life. I remember when I served as a youth director at a church for three years. Things had been going very well in the ministry. We were planted there, serving, loving the Lord and His people. The Spirit of God was actively at work. And then TRANSITION. My wife no longer felt a part of that fellowship of believers. For some time I continued to serve and lead the youth but there came a point where I had to sit down with my pastor and let him know that I was stepping down from all ministry and we were leaving the church altogether. This began a very difficult season of transition in our lives. It would be about eighteen months before we were replanted by God in another church body and into the work of the ministry. But it was during this time I remember just crying out to God. Knowing the deep call and desires He had placed in my heart but yet so discouraged at the same time as we were transitioning and trying to discern the will of God for our lives. I'm sure Abram went through this during his time of transition.

Be encouraged, my brothers and sisters. Without change we are left with just that. No change. We must understand both the heart of God and the leading of the Spirit of God during our transition seasons. Times of transition can seem like you are wandering through a remote wilderness with a compass trying to decide which way to go next. But know that He will be faithful to get you where you need to be. Perhaps even right now you are in a season of transition and change. Maybe it is from one church to another, one ministry to another, or one place of employment to another. Perhaps you are still mourning and grieving the death of someone you loved so dearly. All that once was has been seemingly stripped away from you. And without warning!

Whatever the change is, God will supply just what you need to get you through it. Beloved, take heart in your season of transition. God fulfilled His promises to Abram. And He will fulfill His promises to you! With confidence, I can tell you He brought my family and me into a wonderful, spiritually wealthy place. But it does not happen without TRANSITION.

ABRAHAM

POSSESSING THE PROMISE

DAY 3

And the LORD visited Sarah as He had said,

and the LORD did for Sarah as He had spoken.

For Sarah conceived and bore Abraham a son in his old age,

at the set time of which God had spoken to him.

—Genesis 21:1-2 NKJV

Abram was no longer Abram, but now Abraham! He was a changed man! Abram turned Abraham was transformed and changed by the power of God. Just like you whose lives have been invaded by the Spirit of God and made new in Jesus Christ! But what we must understand and realize is the work God did in Abraham did not happen overnight but over many years. Just like the promise God made to Abraham concerning his son Isaac did not happen rapidly, but took many years to come to fruition.

God spends quality time shaping and transforming His servants both in character and in teaching them to trust Him and walk by faith. When God gives you and me a specific promise, the Lord will put us through His process to prepare us to possess the promise. Do you want to possess the promises of God for your life? Then you must be willing to submit to the Lord's process of preparation in order to receive them. There is no way around it. There is no quick subway you can take. No overnight flight to your Promised Land. There must be the allotted time in each of our lives to give time for the Holy Spirit to do what He does best in us. Nothing is wasted by the Lord. Every hour, every day, each month we are confronted with God-designed circumstances that are intended to shape us into fit men and women of God. Men and women who can be trusted to handle and have in possession the things God has promised us. When we have submitted to God's processes in our lives there comes the day when what God has revealed to us will become a reality and will be manifested for our eyes to see! Oh, what a glorious day! The vision is for a set time. Though you may have to wait for it, it will surely come! God will perform His Word!

Abraham and Sarah had a precious promise from God that they would bear a son even in their old age. From the moment God gave the promise time seemed to go on and on and on with no realization of the promise. Abraham and Sarah entered into a season of desperation. They began to try and possess the promise of God by making plans in the flesh. As the years went on the likelihood of what God said would happen seemed to be a fleeting, far-fetched idea somewhere off in the distance. Surely too much time had passed for God to be faithful to His Word. In the natural they were right. They were both old in age and long past the time of bearing children. But the God we serve is a supernatural God of power and might and He works outside the dimension of natural ability. The Word He speaks He plans to fulfill in just the right time and season. Perhaps you are in this type of season currently. You have received some glorious promise from the Lord that He has revealed to you by His Word and by His Spirit. And now you are in the wilderness of waiting. It has been said by one preacher, "Those who wait upon the Lord, will wait and wait and wait." God is not the One who is in a hurry. Often it is us, you and I, who think we know best when we are ready to enter our Promised Land. We often run ahead of God with great intentions but only to our own harm. But it is God who is full of infinite wisdom. It is the Lord whose thoughts and ways are high above ours. It is Jesus Christ, our loving King, who sees the beginning to the end of our lives. I want to encourage you with this word from the Lord: If He said it, He will do it. If He birthed the desire in your heart, He will bring that desire to pass. And when all around you seems to speak against the promises of God for your life you can be sure of this: ***"He who calls you is faithful, who also will do it"*** **(1 Thessalonians 5:24 NKJV).**

ABRAHAM

LEAVING A LEGACY

DAY 4

Then Abraham gave up the ghost,

and died in a good old age, an old man, and full of years;

and was gathered to his people.

—Genesis 25:8 KJV

Abraham had walked with the Lord. Abraham was a man who encountered the glorious presence of God. He had raised up his family in the ways of God. He had experienced the faithfulness of God firsthand, receiving what the Lord had promised him and Sarah. From the peak of Mount Moriah overlooking the valley below, Abraham had counted the cost to follow His God. He knew the pain of being asked by God to sacrifice that which he loved so dearly. Abraham had fulfilled God's plan and his purpose for being on the earth. Now, his appointed time had come to go home and be with the Lord. **Genesis 25:8 tells us, "Then Abraham gave up the ghost, and died in a good old age, an old man, and full *of years*; and was gathered to his people"** (KJV, emphasis mine). Although Abraham died in the physical, the spiritual legacy he left behind would exceed his largest imagination. A legacy left behind that would leave a lasting impact on many generations to come! Abraham's faith and obedience would earmark a host of generations who would be inspired to fully follow and obey God despite the cost.

Let us also remember through the life of Abraham that a life full of years is most definitely not a life without its heartaches, its learning

19

experiences, its trials, and even its wilderness seasons. Abraham had been through every season of life and he had this testimony: he was a man of faith who heard the voice of God and obeyed. In our natural way of thinking one would think a life lived smoothly and without problems would produce the greatest legacy, but it is not so. There is a personal cost to leaving behind such a legacy. There is no such thing as a "cheap" godly legacy.

The question is: are we willing to pay the price to have the same testimony? What kind of legacy do we desire to leave behind? Right now your faith is being tried. Your ability to trust God and obey even when it doesn't make sense is being tested. The hardships and the painful blows to your heart that cause you to doubt the goodness of God are in all actuality meant to stretch and bring your faith in the Lord to a place of maturity. Just as in the life of Abraham, your test will become your testimony. Your mess will become your message. And your life in its fulfillment will become your legacy in Jesus Christ to the glory of God. The Spirit of God will take the legacy you leave behind and He will impact the lives of many people and inspire them to rise up and become those mighty men and women of God that He has destined for them to become. So do not lose heart in the wildernesses of life. It is in those places your legacy is built one day at a time, one trial at a time, even one moment at a time. *"Only one life to live, twill soon be past. Only what's done for Christ shall last."* These are the well-known words of C.T. Studd, a missionary to China in the nineteenth century. And oh, how so true that we are given one life, with one opportunity to leave behind a lasting legacy in the Lord and for the generations to come.

ISAAC

DIGGING DEEP

DAY 5

And Isaac digged again the wells of water, which they had digged

in the days of Abraham his father; for the Philistines had stopped

them after the death of Abraham: and he called their names after

the names by which his father had called them.

—Genesis 26:18 KJV

Isaac had grown up in the household of faith. Even unto the death of Abraham his father, Isaac witnessed firsthand Abraham's faith, obedience, and ability to trust God even when it didn't make sense. Isaac himself being the promised seed to Abraham and Sarah was now in turn to carry the torch of their faith and continue what they had left behind. It was time for Isaac to rise up and be the man God had called him to be. But in order for that to happen something drastic had to happen. Some major changes would need to occur. The wells once dug by Abraham his father were now filled with the dirt of the Philistines. In order for the water to flow freely again the dirt would need to be removed and the wells restored once again to a place of usefulness.

Here we find a very clear picture and application for you and me. If you and I want to stay in the flow of God's Spirit then we like Isaac must go back and once again dig out the wells full of dirt and debris. Sin, compromise, and the enemy (Philistines) who work so tirelessly to keep our wells filled with dirt will do anything to see us settle for wells that are not fully operational and producing the fresh water of God's Spirit. Consider that a well outwardly

21

can look fully functional. It can appear to be in good working order. But it is not until you drop down the bucket to pull up fresh water that you can tell the health status of that well. There came a point when Isaac recognized the dire need to see these wells in operation again and the Lord will also bring you and me to that precious place of recognizing we need the wells full of His living water to flow once again in our lives.

Right now many of you who are reading these words are in this very place. And it just so happens that God has led you to this point in your journey that He might once again fill you to overflowing with the power of the Holy Spirit. It might even be that right now in this moment God seems distant and it has been so long since you have experienced His manifest presence in your life. But I would rather conclude just the opposite that God is nearer than you think, and right now He is drawing you into a deeper place of intimacy with Himself. He is teaching you to thirst for His living water, to thirst for His presence. He is allowing you to see the uselessness and vanity of dirt-filled wells, in order that you might turn back to Him and drink from the only well that is not polluted with the things of this world. Even now there are many wells all about us. But there is only *one* well that truly satisfies our very souls. There is only *one* well that is pure and flows freely from the throne of God. Could it be in this present hour the Spirit of God is calling you to remove the dirt from your life that is hindering His living water from flowing freely in and through your life?

Digging wells is no easy task and most definitely not for the faint of heart. Isaac labored to ensure the wells were dug properly and flow as they were intended. Digging is laborious, tiresome, and demanding but most rewarding. Do NOT give up! For the one who does not give up digging the promise of fresh water is granted. The same is true for those who will rid themselves of all the dirt that might block the flow of God's Spirit. It may be difficult and require deliberate changes in your life. It may seem you are digging and continue to dig but the Lord Himself will reward your diligence and you will once again see His Spirit flowing powerfully through your life and ministry. Keep digging and dig deep, for the deeper you dig into God's Spirit, the more abundantly His rivers of living water will flow.

ISAAC

VALLEY OF SPRINGS

DAY 6

And Isaac's servants digged in the valley, and found there a well of springing water.

—Genesis 26:19 KJV

"Mountain high, valley low, it is there You restore my soul"
(Anonymous). Isn't it interesting that while Isaac and his servants were still digging wells that it was in the valley place they came across springs of water? We must always remember as we come across verses of Scripture like this that the Lord always has a deeper implication and application for me and you. The Spirit of the Lord always has golden nuggets of truth and revelation that will help us to take the text and make it so relevant to our daily lives. Of course it is NO coincidence that springs of water were found in the valley! Isaac along with any seasoned saint reading these very words knows and understands that the Lord does some of His greatest work in the valley places of our lives.

For most of us, even though we know this truth, we would most gladly prefer to pitch our tents upon the highest mountain of God's presence and if given our own way would never experience adversity or affliction again. But the Lord lovingly says to you and me, come down from the mountain and go down into the valley, for there I will do a work in you by My Spirit that can be done no other way. It is here we come to understand that the mountaintop experiences with the Living God are to prepare us to go down into the lowest valley, for it is there our faith is stretched. Here our character is developed and refined. It is here in the valley places of life that the faithfulness of God becomes engraved on our hearts. How would we come to know and experience the great faithfulness of our God unless He has led us through many troubles? The Enemy of our souls and even our own flesh may scream that God has abandoned us, but those who have gone through the valley learn quite the opposite—that God is ever faithful, even more than we had dreamt. Even in the most difficult and dry places we may find ourselves in, even there the Holy Spirit will in due time refresh us with His springs and renew our souls once again.

Most of us would readily admit we want to grow and mature as followers of Jesus Christ. Many are ready to declare they want more of the anointing of God upon their lives. So many want to walk in the fullness of the Spirit and in the supernatural power of God. But then they wonder in amazement why they are going through so much difficulty and adversity! Reader, take heart. The Lord is doing a marvelous and glorious work in you, and that which seems to be working against you is in reality paving your way forward! The pain you are currently experiencing in the valley is preparing you to draw closer to the promises of God over your life. The valley is preparatory and needful if we will walk into our God-given destinies.

If we would drink of springs in the valley we must also remember this key element: PERSEVERANCE. Those who simply refuse to give up, who simply will not take the easy way out, will experience the Spirit and presence of God in a fresh, new way. We should not just pray to get out of our valley place, but we should pray as to what the Lord desires to work in us through our valley place. From glory to glory we are being transformed by the Spirit of the Lord. The deeper the valley the sweeter the springs we shall find! Right now take a moment even in your hurt to praise God for your valley place. If it were not for where you are right now, you would remain shallow, lacking depth of character and maturity. Get ready: God is enlarging your borders, He is extending your tent pegs, and He is getting ready to refresh you in the "Valley of Springs."

JACOB

DREAMS IN THE NIGHT

DAY 7

So he came to a certain place and stayed there all night, because the sun had set. And he took one of the stones of that place and put it at his head, and he lay down in that place to sleep. Then he dreamed, and behold, a ladder was set up on the earth, and its top reached to heaven; and there the angels of God were ascending and descending on it.

—Genesis 28:11-12 KJV

Jacob had just received the blessing of his father, Isaac. At odds with his brother, Esau, things right now were anything but easy for Jacob. Esau planned to kill Jacob for stealing his birth-bound blessing from Isaac, their father. Jacob was a man on the run, running for his life! Sent out by his parents, Jacob finds himself in Haran. This is the same place where his grandfather Abraham ended up after leaving the land of Ur. Haran, a place defined as dry and desert-like, Jacob now found himself in that wilderness like place. Soon after the sun sets low and night begins to fall. Little did Jacob know it, but he was getting *ready* to have an *encounter* with the Lord that would change the course of his life.

Even many of you right now feel just like Jacob. Maybe you have never had to run for your life, but the pressures that surround you perhaps have caused you to feel that running from your circumstances would be well suitable. Even for some of you right now in a spiritual sense the sun has set in your spirits and the darkness of night has settled in and you are now looking for any glimmer of hope to shine through. Well then, *get ready*, for the *Lord* is that *light* shining through your darkness and *He* is getting *ready* to reveal Himself to you powerfully, even through dreams and visions.

There are times in our lives when the Lord will allow us to experience the darkest of nights but only so that the radiance of His glorious light can shine through. We may seemingly sit in the darkness for a season, but there will come a time as we fix our eyes and our hope upon the Lord that He will break through the dark clouds that loom above and *He* will shine the *Son* into our hearts and spirits once again. Jacob no doubt understood what it was to be in a dark place. And then suddenly and without warning God speaks to Jacob in a dream, reminding Jacob of His abiding presence and steadfast promises.

Some of you need to be reminded that the presence of God is with you. Some of you need to be reminded to cling to the promises of God. The darkness that surrounds us tempts us to believe the lie that God has left the ship and we are attempting to maneuver our ships out on the stormy sea by the strength and wit of our own hands. But no, there is a greater Captain on deck who knows just how to direct our sails and steer our rudders to make it through the darkest storm and safely to land. Not only will God's presence never leave us but what God said concerning our lives, He *will* do, no matter how dark the storm or how long the night.

Here God speaks prophetically to Jacob. He reveals to Jacob in a dream what He will do and that He will see to it that it is accomplished. What has God revealed and spoken to you prophetically? What dreams has He placed within your hearts that seem to have lain dormant for many years? I dare you now to take hold of those God-given dreams and declare them before the Lord. God often will give us dreams and promises long before they will become a reality. The dream may seem like it is ready to die before it is brought to life. But God will resurrect any dream He has given to you and in time

He will move swiftly and suddenly to bring about its fulfillment. I want to encourage you in this very moment to take heart when the night falls upon you. Your darkest wilderness experience is preparing you for God's glorious light to break through. It might just be that God is getting ready to reveal Himself to you, to speak to you, and to give you dreams in the night.

JACOB

FACE-TO-FACE

DAY 8

And Jacob called the name of the place Peniel: for I have seen God face to face.

—Genesis 32:30a KJV

Have you ever been in a situation that gripped your heart with so much fear? With sweat beads rolling down his face and heart pounding in his chest, Jacob surely knew what it was to fear. He was getting ready to stand face-to-face with his own brother, Esau, who at one time vowed to kill Jacob. The fear of not knowing what would happen began to invade Jacobs's thoughts. The anxiousness of the unknown began to take over his emotions. Jacob feared the worst! And isn't that just like us as people to ultimately assume the absolute worst is right around the bend? Yes, we do that quite often. We can be very pessimistic by nature. But aren't you glad that our times and seasons are in the hand of a great God? Aren't you rather blessed that even the seemingly darkest of situations are still in the control of an all-powerful God? Yes, Jacob came to learn this rather quickly and so will you and I in the midst of the trials and turmoil we face. If God be for us, who can be against us?

Even in the midst of what could have been a disastrous run-in with Esau, Jacob was about to have one of the most powerful encounters with the Living God ever recorded in Scripture. Here in Peniel, which literally means "facing God," Jacob would have the privilege of seeing the Lord face-to-face as a man would stand and look at his companion eye-to-eye. How many of us can say we have seen the Lord face-to-face? What an encounter God had planned for Jacob! And where did God plan this encounter? Was it while Jacob was vacationing, taking ease and resting in his comforts? No, it was during the middle of a crisis that God came to him!

So often we magnify the problems in our lives rather than re-membering we serve a mighty God who works for us and on our behalf! Furthermore, through Jacob's circumstance the Lord was using that which seemed to work against Jacob to draw him into a deeper place of intimacy with Himself. Trials and tribulations, pain and problems, are often the catalyst the Lord allows in our lives to awaken within us our deep need for Him. So often, even uninten-tionally, you and I float through life. We get comfortable in our daily routines. We get so used to doing what *we* do that we forget who we really need and depend on. So the Lord may allow a storm or two to enter into our lives. But it is His great love that compels Him to do so, for He knows exactly what is needed to attain our attention and draw our hearts back to Him.

God desired at Peniel to do a deep work of His Spirit in Jacob. The Lord saw the great potential in Jacob to be a mighty man of God, but at the heart level, Jacob was not fully surrendered to God. Jacob was still that supplanter, that deceiver, the conniver who knew how to weasel his way in and out of situations. But God would shake the very foundations of Jacob's heart and strip him down to nothing that He might rebuild him once again. This time Jacob would be known as a man abandoned to God, ready to do His will, His way! Could it be even for you reading this right now that God is bringing you to a place of utter surrender through the trials you have been facing? Could it be even at this very moment the Spirit of God is drawing you to your very own Peniel that you might have a powerful encounter with the Lord unlike anything you have ever experienced? Get ready to see God like never before!

JOSEPH

BITTER BETRAYAL

DAY 9

Now when they saw him afar off, even before he came near them,
they conspired against him to kill him.

—Genesis 37:18 NKJV

Joseph was a young man full of dreams. He was a dreamer, and rightly so! God had given Joseph two powerful prophetic dreams concerning his future and divine destiny. Who wouldn't be excited? Who wouldn't desire to shout it out from the mountaintops? But what Joseph didn't understand in his youthfulness was everything God reveals to us is not always meant to be shared with the world or even those closest to us. We may easily run ahead of God and begin to spout out like an erupting volcano those mysteries and secrets that God intended for only us to know in that time and season. We must learn to stay in step with not only the prophetic word God gives but also the timing of its fulfillment.

While Joseph expected those closest to him to be most encouraging and supportive, what he would find out is that jealousy and bitter betrayal may not be too far from home. Those quickest to turn their backs on us just might be those closest to us. Sometimes jealousy and secret hatred is not so easily seen with the natural eye. People are wonderful at hiding their true motives and agendas. People are some of the greatest pretenders the world has ever known! But put those same people who say they love you in a position to demonstrate who and what they really are and we might be very surprised the ratio of those who are faithful and loyal in comparison with those will readily betray us.

Think with me of our most glorious Savior, Jesus. He ate with Judas. He taught Judas about the kingdom of God. Even in the midst of betrayal, Jesus labeled Judas as his friend. It was one right in the midst of one of his closest circles that would do the most damage to Jesus giving him over to his accusers. The same would prove true with Joseph. They grew up in the same home under their father Israel. They had learned together about the same powerful God that had done wonders in the life of their great-grandfather Abraham and in their grandfather Isaac. But when given the opportunity these brothers of Joseph would prove to be hateful, deceitful, and full of betrayal.

Perhaps in this season of your life or even in past seasons you have experienced the same bitter betrayal. Those who seemed to love and care for you the most turned out to be just the opposite. Going through betrayal can leave us feeling so alone, forsaken, and desolate. But I want to remind you that God's mighty hand never left Joseph's life and His hand will not leave yours either. God started an amazing work in the life of Joseph and the Lord would bring it to fulfillment. Currently the Spirit of the Lord is doing a glorious work in your life and He will finish that which He has started! Others may turn their back on you. They may speak evil of you and accuse you of all kinds of things. They may leave you alone and mark you out as some kind of fool to build up their own egos. They may sell you out to help promote themselves. But the Lord is the lifter of your head, and even in the midst of bitter betrayal you will find One who sticks closer than a brother, the Lord Himself.

JOSEPH

PROMOTED TO PRISON

DAY 10

And Joseph's master took him, and put him into the prison, a place where the king's prisoners were bound: and he was there in the prison.

—Genesis 39:20 KJV

It's one thing to suffer for something we know we did was wrong. But to suffer for doing right and walking in integrity is quite a different story! Joseph was a quality man of God. Full of character, virtue, and excellence, it was not long before the Enemy would try and completely take him out. Isn't it interesting the way this sinful fallen world works? You do what's right and walk in honesty and transparency before the Lord and men and often instead of being rewarded you become the target for all kinds of false accusations and lies from the pit of hell.

It may be even right now you are being erroneously slandered by those you love and once served so dearly and faithfully. You gave them your very best and all that you put your hands to you made doubly sure was done in all sincerity and truthfulness. Yet no matter how much blessing you brought into the lives of others in the end your compensation was not a worthy wage but rather feeling the point of a freshly sharpened knife slowly piercing through the skin on your back.

In the natural realm Joseph had every reason to murmur and complain with the best of them. He could have organized a revolt after being falsely accused for not only something he did not do but also for the fault of his master's wife, who craftily employed her seduction and attempted to lure Joseph into her trap. Joseph had faithfully served Potiphar! He had exercised great character and integrity in all his dealings with his master, Potiphar. Even during the moments of intense trial and temptation when Potiphar's wife attempted to seduce Joseph, he remained faithful! Despite the arrows of false accusation, Joseph was innocent!

Here we see the demonstration of true, godly, Spirit-filled faith. Joseph saw past the natural and looked unto a supernatural God who would use the prison house to bring about promotion in the life of Joseph and ultimately bring him into his divine destiny. The whole time Joseph sat in the prison he used every opportunity to serve his God with excellency, and the favor of God rested upon Joseph. During the tenure of the night while in prison Joseph held onto those powerful prophetic dreams given him by the Lord showing what was to come in his future. If God had told him what he would have to go through to see those dreams become a reality Joseph might have been gripped by fear and backed out all together.

Have you ever considered that the prison you may be currently experiencing is paving the way for your promotion in God? For many of you God has spoken precise prophetic words over your life by His Spirit and yet it seems you remain in the prison house with no glimpse of those promises coming to pass. My beloved brothers and sisters, the prison-like situation you are facing is not necessarily outside of God's glorious plans to bring about His promises for your lives. With great position comes great responsibility. God trains us through the prisons of life so that we might know what is in our hearts and also to prepare us for promotion. I challenge you right now to consider any anointed man or woman of God that you hold in high esteem. You love them, you have such respect for them, you witness firsthand God using them mightily by the power of His Spirit. But have you ever considered what they have been through to get to where they are currently?

Dearly beloved, praise Him in the prison! Proclaim His faithfulness in the prison! For soon, like Joseph, you will see the fruition of the promise come to pass in your life. One day you will look back and see that the prison was to bring you to a place of PROMOTION.

JOSEPH

THE TURNAROUND

DAY 11

"But as for you, you meant evil against me; but God meant it for good, in order to bring it about as it is this day, to save many people alive."

—Genesis 50:20 NKJV

Isn't it wonderful that we serve a heavenly Father who wastes nothing in our lives but uses *all* to fashion us, to transform us, and to shape us into fit servants of God. One pastor has been quoted as saying, "All things are not good, but God works all to the good in our lives." That is the divine sovereignty right before our very eyes. The Enemy of our souls, Satan, and all of his demons may plan evil against our souls, but God will turn their devilish plans around to serve His own purposes!

It had been fourteen years from the time God revealed to Joseph through prophetic dreams what He would do and the realization of those dreams to manifest in the natural. Joseph's betrayal by his brothers, being thrown into a pit, being sold to the Ishmaelites, being thrown into prison for something he didn't even do, all in the natural realm seemed to work against Joseph. But in reality and perhaps not so observable to the physical eye, the supernatural and all-powerful God of Abraham, Isaac, and Jacob was slowly but surely bringing His promises to pass in the life of Joseph.

Often with the prophetic word of God that is spoken over our lives there are seasons of adversity and affliction that come that cause us to doubt the reality of that which the Lord has declared for our lives. It is within human reason that when God says He will perform something in our lives, we have come to believe that we can define step-by-step exactly how the Lord will bring to pass His word. This is our first error. Our responsibility in response to the word of the Lord is not to figure out how it will happen but rather to walk in faith and trust the Lord to do what He said He would do. God is not a man that He should lie nor the son of man that He should repent. What He says He will do and what He has declared no matter what it may look like will happen in His timing and season.

The challenge for you and me is whether we will continue to trust that the Lord truly is working all to the good and the fulfillment of His purposes when all seems to work against us. Some of you reading this right now are contending to keep your faith and trust in God to fulfill His promises. You have heard the word of the Lord and instead of the smooth sailing into those promises you so desire, rather there has been storm after storm, which seems to contradict what God said would happen. *Now* is the time to declare boldly back to the Lord that which He has promised you! There is no turning back now. Only forward movement to step into those prophetic promises given you by God.

A whole nation was preserved through Joseph's obedience. Not only did Joseph receive the blessing and benefit of receiving the promise of God, but God's people as a nation were recipients of those same blessings and benefits. The same is true in our lives. The fulfillment of God's promises in our lives bring the blessings of God into our families, to our friends, even multitudes of people! One day you will look back at all the difficulties you have faced and you will say, that which was meant for evil, God made the great TURNAROUND, working all things to the good bringing about the fulfillment of His promise to me.

MOSES

MADE FOR MORE

DAY 12

Now Moses kept the flock of Jethro his father in law, the priest of Midian: and he led the flock to the backside of the desert, and came to the mountain of God, even to Horeb. And the angel of the LORD appeared unto him in a flame of fire out of the midst of a bush: and he looked, and, behold, the bush burned with fire, and the bush was not consumed.

—Exodus 3:1-2 KJV

It had been forty long, seemingly drawn-out years on the backside of a dry desert. Thoughts of serving God and stepping into His higher calling were now the furthest thing from Moses' mind. It seemed like forever! Surely he must not have heard the voice of the Lord clearly. How could he ever think he was to be a deliverer for a whole nation? And not just for any nation but for Israel, God's chosen people, the very apple of His eye. No, there is no way now! That dream he once had, that passion that once stirred within him, but where was it now? Have you ever had thoughts like that? Dreams that have died. Desires from the Lord unfulfilled. Promises from God that you thought would never come to pass. But just when it seemed that all was lost, God called out to Moses. God commissioned Moses. In that moment, Moses realized that all He endured and went through in this past season was to prepare him for such a time as this. The realization came to Moses that he was made for more.

What Moses did not truly understand during his time in the desert as we often do not understand either is that God was steadily shaping and transforming Moses for his life calling and purpose. How many of you know that God is in the great business of powerfully changing lives? You see, Moses ran into the desert self-confident, somewhat arrogant, and proudly ready for anything that came his way. But Moses came out of that forty-year season in the desert meek, humbled, and stripped of all his former confidences. He would learn that His true source of power and empowerment came only from the Lord.

There is a great stripping and refinement that takes place in our lives when we find ourselves in that desert- and wilderness-like place. For some of you even as you read these words you are in this very season right now. I want to encourage you that perhaps God is stripping some layers of flesh from your inner man that you might be filled with more of Him. In order for you to move to the next level and step into your next season there are some things that you must let go of. It is in the letting go that you become free to embrace all that God has for you in the next portion of your life and ministry. As you do, you are going to sense in this next season such richness from the Spirit of God and a great sense of purpose and destiny!

Isn't it wonderful to know that we weren't created by God to just roam the earth. We weren't made to just earn a paycheck, or to get married, or even just to have children. But each of us were MADE FOR MORE and our great purpose is in knowing Jesus Christ and finding out what the Spirit of God has gifted and graced us to do for the kingdom of God. With that being said, God is deliberate and purposeful on His end in making the necessary changes in us that we might be fit for the call of God. When you find yourself like Moses on the backside of the desert, remember this is a part of God's making and fashioning you that you might be that mighty man or woman of God that He desires for you to be. Truly, you have been MADE FOR MORE!

MOSES

BRUTALLY BOUND

DAY 13

"Ever since I came to Pharaoh as your spokesman, he has been even more brutal to your people. And you have done nothing to rescue them!"

—Exodus 5:23 NLT

Sometimes we mistake the harsh circumstances that hold us bound for a God who does not care, or is cruel, and has no grand master plan or intent to help us out of the bondage we find ourselves in. How far from the truth! Though Israel still lay brutally bound to Pharaoh and the Egyptians, God was working in the background and in the shadows setting them up for their greatest victory yet! Howbeit that which held them down would soon turn out to work for their deliverance. Hallelujah, what a mighty God we serve!

One of the greatest truths you and I can hear is that the Lord has a plan of deliverance for our lives as well! Isn't that the very reason why Moses was raised up by the Lord, for such a time as this? Yes, Moses through the power of God would prove to be a mighty deliverer for God's people. But we also have a glorious deliverer and His name is Jesus! Sometimes we feel that the heavy shackles that hold us down will never be loosed! It could be depression. It could be fear and anxiety. It could well be some area or sin in our lives we have yet to overcome. But Jesus Christ breaks every chain! There is no bondage in our lives that cannot be broken through the power of the cross of Jesus Christ.

When we come to Jesus and receive Him, He provides a wonderful salvation for our souls, changing our eternal destination. But even after we have come to Him, He is still in the business of breaking those things that hinder our forward progress! What has held you BRUTALLY BOUND must bow to the name of Jesus!

Surely Moses felt desperate in this situation. He knew what God had said He would do, but in the natural realm it surely seemed the condition of God's people had grown worse rather than better. But here God is setting the stage. It's as if God's people are behind the curtain just before it opens to a large awaiting audience. And just when the time is right God will have that curtain open to show just how mighty and faithful He truly is to His people. God does not move ahead early and He certainly is NEVER late. He is an on-time God. Right now for many of you reading this God has already set the stage for you. The victory has already been won, the deliverance already been provided, and God is seeing you through that which seems to hold you bound to a glorious freedom! In His timing the curtain will open in your lives as a testimony to those around you of the supernatural power of God at work on your behalf.

Even up to the moment the Spirit of God led me to receive Jesus Christ my life had been filled with people, places, and things that held me bound. But let me tell you as the Word of God tells us that where the Spirit of the Lord is there is freedom! Sometimes that which binds us is of our own doing and because of personal choices and sometimes it is quite the opposite. Whatever it might be, remember today along with me that our God has a great plan of deliverance for anything we may be experiencing. Even when the circumstances scream the complete opposite, let us believe together that the Lord will break that which binds us and lead us out into His wonderful freedom.

MOSES

GO FORWARD

DAY 14

*And the LORD said to Moses, "Why do you cry to Me? Tell the chil-
dren of Israel to go forward."*

—Exodus 14:15 NKJV

It has been said that there is only one direction in the kingdom
of God, and that is FORWARD! Who hasn't had a past where there is
some degree of regret? Who can take an honest audit of their lives
and declare in good conscience they have made all the best decisions,
used all of the time granted them wisely, and made the most out of
every opportunity? There is not a one in the household of God who
has not been redeemed from a life of sin and self! That is the beauty
of the wondrous cross of Jesus Christ! It takes undeserving, imperfect
people like you and me and takes all the messes of our past and paves
the way onward for a glorious future in God, so that we might move
forward into our destiny.

It is not only past regrets that may attempt to keep us from moving
forward, but it may be fear that has gripped our hearts. Imagine you
are an Israelite following the Lord and the leadership of Moses. You
are standing in the face of this great Red Sea. It is quite easy to tell
others to have great faith and trust in God, but when you yourself are
standing in face of something so enormous and with an angry mob
of Egyptians behind you the command from God is quite clear: GO
FORWARD! There is no other direction to take!

41

The deliverance God provided from the Egyptians was quite glorious, but that didn't mean God's people were to slow down their momentum! They were to accelerate FORWARD, allowing nothing to hinder their progression. When we came to Jesus Christ we were given new life and made into *new* creatures. We have been made an abode for the indwelling of His presence, the very Spirit of the Living God. One of the greatest miracles we bear witness to is the power of God to change a life. The Holy Spirit comes in and begins to change our desires. He changes our life's purpose and direction. He brings us into alignment to the will of God for our lives that we might fulfill our heavenly calling and mandate from God.

But along the way we falter, we fall, and we fail at times. That which we said we would never do again, we do again. Those words we promised to never say again, we so quickly speak. That thing we vowed to never indulge in again, we run to in the moment of trial and temptation. So what do we do when we fall? I suggest we fall FORWARD and do what the writer of Proverbs instructs us to do. Proverbs 24:16a in the Amplified Bible tells us, **"For a righteous man falls seven times and rises again."** The position we have won in Christ does not permit us to stay fallen! We can rise up once again and continue to go forward.

I sense this is a very applicable word for many who read this. No matter how bad you have failed or how awful you have faltered, I want to encourage you with this word in this moment to continue pressing forward! So many times in my walk with the Lord my own sin and failure has caused me to become discouraged and quite weary. But the Lord has always encouraged me to get up and go forward with Him! Right now, in this moment, let's agree together, that which has been done is in the past, now lies before us a glorious future and hope in Jesus Christ. Let us GO FORWARD!

MOSES

SEA OF SITUATIONS

DAY 15

*And Moses stretched forth his hand over the sea, and the sea
returned to his strength when the morning appeared; and the
Egyptians fled against it; and the Lord overthrew the Egyptians in
the midst of the sea.*

—Exodus 14:27 KJV

There are just some situations we face in life that we have no idea
how we are going to get through. Where is the breakthrough we so
desperately need? One day life can seem so wonderful and full of bliss
and the next the painful realities of living in a sinful, fallen world can
seemingly slap us in the face. The Israelites experienced a powerful
deliverance by the mighty hand of God and under the leadership of
Moses. But having been brought out of Egypt there still remained this
gaping and daunting task that lay before them of crossing the Red Sea.

The same can be all so true for you and me as well. We've come
to experience some mighty move of God's hand in our lives and the
next thing we know, we are faced with some enormous situation we
wished we were not dealing with at the moment. Even as you read this
many of you may be going through the most difficult trial of your lives
but I want to encourage you that the larger the trial and situation, the
greater deliverance the Lord has prepared. The grander the problem,
the more the borders of our faith and trust in the Lord are enlarged.

What situation do you find yourself in today? Is it the death of a loved one? Could it be betrayal on the part of someone you loved and trusted? Or is it possibly some great financial need? It could well be some sickness or ailment in your body. For some you may be going through or have gone through the painful process of divorce. The sea of possible situations is endless. Again, no matter the problem, our God will meet us in our need in proportion to what we are going through. There is no mountain too high, no ocean too deep, where His power and providence cannot meet us right where we are at.

I remember when my wife and I brought our precious daughter, Hannah, home from the hospital. It was no more than two weeks later that she developed a cough that caught our attention. It was no normal cough that accompanies a common cold. Within hours of bringing her to the doctors we learned she had developed a condition called dilated cardiomyopathy. Basically this is a form of congestive heart failure. Suddenly, we found ourselves basically living at the hospital. Every question begins to run through your head at this point. But I made a decision in my heart to trust God. If He had brought me through so many situations before, He would do it again! And the same is true of you! Praise God our daughter is healed now and no longer on medications, but we give all the honor and glory to the One is our Healer!

The parting of the Red Sea reveals so much more to us than meets the eye. It shows you and me to what great extent God will go to rescue His own. Even if God has to part the Red Seas of our lives, He will come to our aid and help us get through any and every situation. Sometimes we stand facing a SEA OF SITUATIONS, not knowing whether the waves will come crashing down on us if we take another step. But the One who bids us to come through the SEA will SEE to it that we make it through to the other side.

MOSES

CONSTANT COMPLAINERS

DAY 16

Then the people complained and turned against Moses. "What are
we going to drink?" they demanded.

—Exodus 15:24 NLT

Nothing is so effective at quenching the Spirit in our lives than being around others who are ungrateful and consistently unthankful. Some people are so blinded by their own pessimism it is surprising they can even see enough to walk one foot in front of them let alone recognize the many blessings from the hand of God in their lives. Nothing seems harder than to try to please a person who always seems to be in a place of discontentment.

At this time Israel was such a people. How could such a nation as Israel forget so quickly the goodness of their God? How could they be so rebellious and treat their leader Moses with such disrespect? They had become CONSTANT COMPLAINERS, unable to be pleased and carrying with them a dishonorable sense of entitlement! What about the great deliverance they had just experienced? What other nations or people could honestly say that the God of the universe had parted the Red Sea for them? And yet when they didn't get what they wanted right when they wanted it they immediately manifested what they truly were: a group of CONSTANT COMPLAINERS! What they needed was a massive shift in their perspective and a renewal in how they viewed their God!

Such is true in the lives of many of you who are reading this. There are those in your lives whom you have gone above and beyond to bless. You have invested your time, your treasure, your very being into the lives of others. Yet sadly, many who receive our best hold what we have imparted to them in such low esteem. It's as if they have forgotten that the words "thank you" are still a part of our vocabulary. One of the most powerful attitudes we can have in the Christian life is to be thankful both to God and towards others! An attitude of gratitude goes a long way! Take heart, my beloved brothers and sisters. If anyone knows about dealing with unthankful and ungrateful people, it is the Lord!

This leaves us with the most obvious and rhetorical question. Shouldn't thankfulness be the constant attitude in our hearts? Haven't we learned to be thankful even when things are not necessarily going the way we would like? In the natural in accordance with our human element, it is normal to desire to complain. But it is the Spirit of the Lord within us that reminds us and brings us to a place of remembrance of all the Lord has been to us and all He has done for us. Even through the difficult and wilderness place in our lives we have more than enough reason to give God praise and to be thankful towards His holy Name.

Moses experienced firsthand the bitter arrows of constant complaint thrown at him. He knew well the deep hurt of having those he cared for turn so quickly on him. But God always vindicated His servant Moses. Perhaps some of you are experiencing sorrow over those you have poured your life into. It could be your own children. It could be a close friend or companion. It could be those in the work of the ministry that God has entrusted to your care. You've given them your very best and all they have done is complained and shown a lack of gratitude. I want to encourage you with this word from the Lord. When people overlook our labor, we serve a God who notices every act of service whether seemingly big or small. Even though you might be in the presence of CONSTANT COMPLAINERS, soon and very soon you will experience the rich reward that only God can give for being His faithful servant.

MOSES

WORN AND WEARY

DAY 17

*But Moses' hands grew weary, so they took a stone and put it under
him, and he sat on it, while Aaron and Hur held up his hands, one
on one side, and the other on the other side. So his hands were steady
until the going down of the sun.*

—Exodus 17:12 ESV

The call to leadership is clearly not an easy call. Here we see the
transparency of Moses, who was rather tired at this point. This should
bring great encouragement to leaders in the body of Christ. Sometimes
we feel that we must take on the role of a superhero! The kind that
never get tired, never get discouraged, never feel a sense of defeat.
Honestly speaking Moses was one of the greatest leaders of all time.
Having led a nation of about three million people, as pertaining to
leadership in the kingdom of God, Moses was a general! If Moses
experienced what is was to be WORN AND WEARY, we can identify
with Moses and be encouraged by his example and testimony. This
does not make us less impactful or effective as leaders—it means we
are human. Any real strength we receive to do the work of God comes
from the power of the Holy Spirit as He dwells within us and also
comes upon us.

In Exodus 17 we are onlookers straight into a battle scene. There
is a war going on between Israel and Amalek. War is not glamorous
but sometimes needful to bring us into a place of victory. Sometimes

we have to say things just as they are. The battle is very real and can leave us feeling WORN AND WEARY. Some of you reading this right now are feeling the intensity of the battle. For some it may seem that one problem runs right into the next problem and it leaves you asking, "When will it ever end?" Like Moses your hands have grown weary through the battle and you are more than ready for the extra support to be sent in to your aid.

One thing we must understand is Amalek is a picture or a type of the flesh. What we see is a battle not just between Israel and Amalek, but also between the believer and the flesh. Warring with our flesh can be most tiresome! But, praise God He has given us a support, a supernatural power. The Lord has given us someone outside of ourselves to do for us what we cannot do alone in and of ourselves. And that is the person of the Holy Spirit! While Aaron and Hur can well represent those fellow saints God sends into our walk for personal help when it is needed, we also have a picture of the very Spirit of the Living God who in the midst of the battle gives us supernatural and extraordinary strength that energizes our very spirits and brings life to our weary souls. We must take full advantage of the helper provided to us by God, and that is the Lord Himself found in the Person of His Spirit! Yes, for some there is a strength rising within your inner man even as you read this!

One of the most glorious promises to the believer in Jesus Christ is the promise of triumph and victory. Christ defeated Amalek once and for all on the cross. Through His death and resurrection we become partakers of His victory! I want to speak to you personally that no matter how WORN AND WEARY you may feel in this moment, the Lord will be ever faithful to see you through victorious! Not only are we battling our flesh, but we are in a heated spiritual battle where in the realm of the spirit there is a constant war taking place. The Enemy is working hard to keep people blinded to the truth of the gospel and also doing everything he can to keep the people of God from being powerful influencers and world changers for Jesus Christ and the kingdom of God.

God gave Moses and Israel the win over Amalek, and He will do the same for you! Moses then built an altar to worship the Lord and named it Jehovah Nissi meaning, "the Lord is my banner." Right now I want to encourage each of you that read this to build your own altar even in the midst of the battle and begin to worship the Lord for the victory He has already promised you. While in the natural you may be WORN AND WEARY, you will soon experience the Lord wave His banner of victory over your life. New strength is rising, a new day is coming, a new season lies ahead. Let us go onward and upward to victory!

MOSES

ON EAGLES' WINGS

DAY 18

Ye have seen what I did unto the Egyptians, and how I bare you on eagles' wings,

and brought you unto myself.

—Exodus 19:4 KJV

Eagles are another one of God's most magnificent creations. One of their most dynamic features is their ability to carry more weight on their backs than any other bird! How fitting for the Lord to reference the eagle! The Lord was willing to take the weight and burden upon Himself to see His people through to a place of victory and safety in Him. Isn't it wonderful that we do not have to carry the weight of all our burdens? But we may cast them upon the One who is able to bear them. Not even an earthly pharaoh in all of his worldly power, with all of his Egyptian followers, could stop the God of the universe from delivering His people. And nothing or no one can stop the Lord's powerful hand from moving on your behalf!

Every one of us is in need of the deliverance that only God can provide. Each of us has experienced being in bondage in some form. We have had and still have various forms of pharaohs in our lives that God desires to deliver us from. The Lord knew the sorrows of His people. He understood well the baggage they were carrying not only physically but also in their hearts. Sometimes we consider the delays of God to be His denials. In this we are very mistaken. In the waiting we may doubt God's design for deliverance. But it would not be long for the manifestation of God's dealings with His people to surface. *Every chain that held His people down would be broken!* Every shackle that held them bound would be loosed! And in their waiting, suddenly their God would rescue them, carry their burdens, and swiftly as the eagle, carry them to safety! And your God will come through for *you* as well!

Eagles are also known for their keen vision. It is noted that some species of eagles can see over three-and-a-half times better than the human eye. Eagles are more than able to see, and not just what is up close and personal but also that which is off in the distance. The Lord saw His people in their most miserable condition. But He also saw them in their future state of complete freedom! Many of you right now need to hear this word from the Lord. The current state which you find yourselves in is not the way it will always be! God sees you not only in the pain you are experiencing but also in the praise you will give to Him because of His deliverance in your lives! Pharaoh falsely assumed He would always hold captive the people of God. But he was sadly mistaken. Likewise that which seems to hinder your forward progress will be removed with the help of God's Spirit, and for some suddenly! Not only does the Lord see the destination He is bringing us to, but He also sees the details in getting there. That is why we must not only trust Him but walk in obedience to Him for He has promised to carry us onward to victory.

Consider the strength in the back of an eagle. The eagle bears the brunt of the work. Those being carried receive the benefits of the eagle's labor. And the same is true in our lives. The battle belongs to the Lord! He carries the real weight. The Lord gives us the power by His Spirit to do what we cannot do in and of ourselves! We are blessed by the Lord and His daily benefits. The cross of Jesus Christ has paid it all and paved the way to bring us out of our bondage and into His freedom. We have been carried by the One who first carried His cross. Like the eagle He has borne our sin, borne our sorrows, and brought us to Himself.

MOSES

MOUNTAIN OF GOD

DAY 19

But Moses said to the Lord, *"The people cannot come up to Mount Sinai; for You warned us, saying, 'Set bounds around the mountain and consecrate it.'"*

—Exodus 19:23 NKJV

Have you ever stood at the base of mountain and stood in awe of its vastness? It is one thing to view a mountain in a picture, but quite another to stand before one physically. Mountains in the Scriptures can represent the great impossibilities in our lives that can be removed only by the powerful hand of God by faith. Mountains also signify those special intimate encounters with the Living God. Here, Mount Sinai represents that place where God would personally hand over to Moses His laws that were to govern the people of God. The law representing God's standards was to be the authority by which the Israelites lived.

But as we look a little deeper, Mount Sinai also represents that MOUNTAIN of impossibility in our lives to keep the standard of God! This is a word specifically for those who always are giving their best spiritually speaking to please God in all things and yet feel like they are failing. You are like the world's best highbar jumper! But as much as you try you can never reach that height of perfection you so desire! Be encouraged, for the Lord calls us up to His MOUNTAIN not just to give us rules to follow but rather to have deep intimacy and communion with us! He is well aware of your shortcomings and setbacks.

He knows your deep desire to be pleasing to Him in all things. He knows how easily sin can beset us.

The Lord did not give us His Law in His Word because He demands or even expects perfection. For some of you reading this you need to hear this Word from the Lord. As much as God wants you to be free from sin and live in a holy manner before Him, He knows that we are incapable of reaching such a standard as Sinai. Perfectionism can quickly turn into legalism, which in turns quenches the Spirit of God. Be encouraged by the Lord! Rest in Him! Walk in the power of His Spirit! He will help you to overcome those things in your lives that are setting you back spiritually! You are an overcomer in Jesus Christ! That is why we are now under grace, for grace enables the believer not to live any kind of way but to live right before the Lord.

Just like Moses, you and I are being called up to the MOUNTAIN OF GOD! He is drawing us near! He is bidding us to climb His mountain and get close to Him. Even for some of you reading this you are sensing the Spirit of the Lord wooing you and drawing you near. Being on the mountain with God is the best place to be! Even in the wilderness, Moses amazingly runs right into Mount Sinai and is called up the mountain by God. My beloved brothers and sisters, even in the midst of your wilderness, do not be surprised when you suddenly are called up the mountain by God. Some of the most difficult and dry seasons of our lives are just preparing us to climb up the mountain and experience the Lord in a fresh, new way. Perhaps you are in this type of season right now. Be encouraged, your wilderness will lead you to the mountain of God. The Lord knows just how much we can handle and will not leave us in the wilderness a moment longer than is necessary for our proper spiritual growth and maturity. Soon you will experience a freshness of God's presence and a richness of God's Spirit as He calls you up the mountain, the very mountain of God!

MOSES

JADED BY JEALOUSY

DAY 20

So they said, "Has the LORD indeed spoken only through Moses? Has He not spoken through us also?" And the LORD heard it.

—Numbers 12:2 NKJV

Promotion comes from the Lord! As simple as that may sound for some, God is the One who chooses. He is the One who elevates, and He is the One who orchestrates circumstances and situations to put the right people in the right place at the right time. Moses was such a man, called of God, handpicked by God to lead a whole nation, even a rebellious and unthankful people.

Whenever God graces a person for leadership, there always comes with that territory those who harbor vicious jealousy in their hearts towards that particular leader. Unfortunately, just as it happened to Moses, so it is in the body of Christ today. There are those who are not content to be who God intended for them to be. They are constantly looking to the next servant of God and comparing themselves with that individual. Not only that but often there is an underlying issue of jealousy that begins to build and mount in the heart, until eventually it manifests and exposes itself in some kind of revulsive action.

Moses had been with these people so long and yet after he marries the Ethiopian woman, all of sudden they begin to attack the character and calling of Moses. It started with their criticism of his marriage to this woman and then the floodgates of what was really in their

54

hearts flowed forth. After all, where did Moses get all of this author-ity anyways? Who does he think he is? Does he really believe he is a mouthpiece for the Living God? Is he really a better man of God than any of us? What gives him the right to tell us what to do? The answer to all of these questions is simply this: Moses was called, anointed, empowered, and endued with authority by the highest authority of all, the Lord of lords and King of kings, even Almighty God. But in their hearts layers of jealousy began to peel away, bringing forth their obvious indictment against Moses: Can't God speak through us also?

Some of you reading this right now are perhaps experiencing this very thing in this time and season. You have been graced and anointed by the Spirit of the Lord for some position with authority. But, there are those standing alongside of you who are harboring something inwardly against you that might not be so visible to the natural eye. Time will tell who is genuinely for you and supportive to the call of God on your life. Then for some there are those who are experiencing an all-out launch of attack on their person and character. Why? Because jealousy is in the camp! It's not that you did anything wrong, but on the contrary, it is what they cannot find against you that bothers them! Your integrity and godly conduct actually feed the flame of jealousy that burns in their hearts. One of the greatest trials within the work of the ministry is to find out that those who pretended to be on the frontlines with you could very well be the ones who hold secre-tive jealousy within their hearts. If you are experiencing this presently my beloved brothers and sisters, take heart—the Lord is with you!

God always stands in the gap for not only His people but for those He has called into specific positions of leadership. When people rise up against you, the Lord Himself will also rise to shut down your critics. Oh, they may carry on with their jealous rants for a season, but God will vindicate you and shut them down in their evil pursuits. I believe the Lord would say to you that vengeance belongs to Him. Do not take matters into your own hands but commit all of it into His hands. The Lord will defend His true servants, and in due time those who are jaded by jealousy will see with their very eyes who has been chosen by the Most High, and who has not.

JOSHUA

MELTED HEARTS

DAY 21

And the men of Ai struck down about thirty-six men, for they chased them from before the gate as far as Shebarim, and struck them down on the descent; therefore the hearts of the people melted and became like water.

—Joshua 7:5 NKJV

Have you ever been in the midst of a storm so fierce, a trial so pressing, a difficulty so unimaginable that you felt you were caving in on the inside? Joshua and the nation of Israel had just experienced one of the greatest victories recorded in all of Scripture. Walking in faith and obedience, they were firsthand eyewitnesses to the supernatural power of God at work tearing down the very walls of Jericho! What a glorious victory indeed! God had shown up on behalf of His people once again and performed a mighty miracle to give them the upper hand over their enemies. But now in the midst of their enemies they were faint, weak, and weary. They were defeated, discouraged, and downtrodden. So much so that their hearts were MELTED within them. Have you been there? Are you currently going through something similar?

After each victory we are reminded of the importance of watching carefully over our ways. Remember for every step forward in God the Enemy has a plan of assault against us that he is just waiting to launch. Of course the Enemy is not pleased that we have overcome some area in our lives. He does not want to see us walk in the power of God's Spirit and rise above every obstacle! So he works constantly against us especially after our sudden victories to try and trip us up. We have become like target boards for his fiery darts and he is relentless! After every win in the kingdom of God the guard must be set for there are more battles to be won!

Perhaps some of you have just experienced the mighty hand of God working on your behalf. He has brought you through some pressing trial. The Spirit of God has aided you in overcoming some besetting sin. But as fast as you gained momentum in the Lord it seems the victory celebration has been cut short by enormous amounts of pressure all around you. The Israelites had gained the upper hand over Jericho for sure. But before going straight in to take over Ai they forgot one but most needful detail: to inquire of the Lord! They assumed how God would work yet they were mistaken and paid the price for their error. They went from REJOICING hearts to MELTED hearts.

Even so, in the midst of a massive mistake we find the mercy and grace of God. As a father lovingly teaches and disciplines his children so the Lord chastens those whom He loves! The hearts of God's people had MELTED from their sudden defeat, but the Lord would raise them up once again. He was not done with them. He had not forsaken His people, and He has not forgotten about you either. Sometimes the Lord in His love for us will allow us to experience the pain that comes with making decisions outside of His will for our lives. But, it is to teach us so that we might learn for our future progress in the Lord.

And then there are some of you who may be suffering at the hand of someone else. Achan brought about defeat and death even upon his own family because of his disobedience to the word of the Lord. They were not directly at fault and yet they still were hugely impacted by the decision of one man. Sin in the camp never just affects one person but can spread rapidly to those around us in our homes, in our churches, and even further abroad.

Perhaps your heart is melting as the Enemy is chasing you down just like Ai chased down the Israelites. I want to encourage you with this word from the Lord. When your heart is weak, remember that the Spirit of God will once again renew and strengthen your hearts. Failure is not permanent and the Lord will bring you into a place of triumph once again. Where your hearts once melted with fear and anxiety, His peace and His presence will flood your hearts and spirits again!

GIDEON

SMALL YET STRONG

DAY 22

And the LORD looked upon him, and said, Go in this thy might, and thou shalt save Israel from the hand of the Midianites: have not I sent thee? And he said unto him, Oh my Lord, wherewith shall I save Israel? behold, my family is poor in Manasseh, and I am the least in my father's house.

—Judges 6:14-15 KJV

Surely the Lord must've made a mistake. God must not have thoroughly thought things through before calling upon Gideon for such a noble task! There must have been multitudes of men more suitable for the job. Do you ever feel like that? This may also be what Gideon was thinking, but the Lord thought otherwise! The Lord loves to use the weak, those whom the world would bypass and set on the shelf. Those are exactly the ones God calls and chooses to accomplish His purposes in the earth. Remember those whom God chooses are not those the world would ordinarily pick.

Midian was now heavily oppressing God's chosen people. Time and time again God would bring about a great deliverance for His people and time and time again they would run back to their sin and idolatry. But our God is a faithful God who never forsakes His people. Something was to be done. Change was imminent. Transition was coming and that quickly. The time had come for Gideon to break out of his shell and become the leader God had called him to be. God would use Gideon mightily to once again deliver his people out of the hands of their enemies. But upon God's calling Gideon immediately exposes his insecurities by responding to God with a question: How could I possibly be a deliverer for this nation?

Some of you right now are feeling just like Gideon. The call of God upon your life is so heavy and undeniable, but you are struggling with the task that lies before you. I want to encourage you with this: When the Lord calls a man or woman and gives him or her a vision for what He desires to accomplish, the task is always much bigger than the servant of God. In fact, because it seems impossible actually verifies that the vision is from God. If we were able to accomplish the work of God so easily we may as well take the credit for ourselves. But God gives us a much larger vision for what He will do and with His strength and by His Spirit He will enable us to see the vision through. Then, He will get all the glory!

Often those God calls are heavily criticized by those around them. Even some that are closest to you will not be as supportive to the call of God on your life as you would think or want them to. But be encouraged: when God raises up a man or a woman for a specific task, the Lord will surround that person with who and what they need when they need it and no one will stop it! Do not be so easily discouraged by who may not support you currently as you step into new levels of ministry. It's not so important that everyone support you, only that the right people do. Along with the giftings He has placed on the inside of you He will also place just the right people around you to help the vision become a reality. Even when you are starting out small, you are still strong in God! For it is His Spirit at work within you to see the work through to completion. Do not despise the day of small beginnings! What starts out as seemingly small will not end up that way. In your lives and in your ministries what begins small may very well end up having enlarged borders, even greater than you can imagine!

Gideon was faced with a daunting task and he would need to be obedient to the voice of the Lord to defeat Midian God's way. God gives Gideon a strategic plan for victory. And what does God do? He raises up a small army of three hundred men to overtake the Midianites. The Lord's thoughts are not our thoughts and His ways are above our ways. What we may think is the best in the natural is often proved wrong by our supernatural God! Today, be encouraged with this word from the Lord. Remember His power at work within you. Remember His abiding presence in your lives. Bring even the little you have and marvel how the Lord will turn it around and use it mightily! You are SMALL YET STRONG!

RUTH

NO TURNING BACK

DAY 23

But Ruth replied, "Don't ask me to leave you and turn back.
Wherever you go, I will go; wherever you live, I will live. Your people
will be my people, and your God will be my God."

—Ruth 1:16 NLT

"I have decided to follow Jesus. No turning back, no turning back."

—Sadhu Sundar Singh

More than just lyrics to a song, this could well describe the bold decision made by Ruth after going through one of the most devastating trials one could go through. Ruth, whose husband had just died, could have used that as a catalyst to run further away from God. But what we find is quite the opposite. Ruth, even in all of the pain she was experiencing, pressed into the Lord and even went so far as to leave her old life completely behind in exchange for the new life she would find in God. Little did Ruth realize she was beginning to walk out her very destiny as what would unfold in the days ahead for her would far exceed any dreams she had for herself. Ruth was a woman of destiny who purposed to live her life for the Lord!

Ruth, whose name means "friendship," had given up her loyalty to the world and past life to partner with Naomi and ultimately God Himself. Leaving Moab behind Ruth's eyes were fixed on the path God set before her. Behold, the Lord was doing a new thing. She was now a new woman. The direction of her life had now taken a swift and sudden change. Even as the wind blows, it was no longer the winds of this world blowing her to and fro and every which way but rather the wind of God's Spirit that would now lead her and bring her into God's divine purposes for her life. But this major transition in Ruth's life did not come easily but rather in the face of much pain and difficulty. Some of you reading this need to be reminded that some of the most blessed seasons of our lives are preceded by pain and difficulties. The afflictions you are currently in could well indicate the season of blessedness that is soon to come. Take heart and keep pressing forward.

Death has a way of slapping each one of us in the face. We live our daily lives doing what we do sometimes, thinking that things will never change. And then death knocks on the door and suddenly we realize very quickly that our lives truly are as a vapor—here one day and gone the next. It's one thing to lose a close friend or even a family member. But Ruth had lost her spouse. The second half of her soul was now gone. Yet the truth is very clear. Although painful, this circumstance thrusted Ruth forward into making a decision to wholeheartedly follow the Lord. The pain in your lives may not immediately reveal any good thing. But often the Lord will allow us to experience difficulties, especially if it will draw us into a deeper relationship with Himself.

In January of 2014, I was scheduled to minister at a pastors and leaders conference in Bogota, Colombia, in South America. The day before I was scheduled to leave I was having breakfast with my wife and three children. After breakfast we decided to go and check on my wife's mother, Elsie. She had not been answering her phone and we were concerned. Upon arrival we knew something was wrong when we saw her car parked in front of her apartment. Our worst fear became a reality as we discovered she had passed away suddenly and without warning. There were so many questions to be answered. How did this happen? Ultimately we have to resolve to put what we cannot understand into the hands of Almighty God.

Life has a way of being consistently inconsistent. But like Ruth, even in the midst of inconvenient and painful circumstances, for you and me there is NO TURNING BACK! Ruth's life proved and manifested the favor of God as He would bring her into a glorious future in Him. Soon all the heartache she had endured would be behind her and she would walk in the newness prepared for her by God. Likewise concerning you, God is using your difficulty to thrust you into your destiny. There is NO TURNING BACK!

BARREN AND BITTER

DAY 24

And she was in bitterness of soul, and prayed unto the L{\scriptsize ORD}, and wept sore.

—1 Samuel 1:10 KJV

It is one thing to want something, and quite another to have a desire. There is a reason why the writer of Proverbs stated in **Proverbs 13:12b, "a desire fulfilled is a tree of life!" NIV.** Reason being, a desire speaks much deeper than something we may simply want. Rather, the word desire speaks of an intense longing or craving that will not go away so easily. Often what we desire is what presses us on until we receive that which we are so desperate for.

Hannah was such a woman. She was a woman of desire. For some time Hannah's heart had ached the desire of women—to give birth to a child. So much so that it brought Hannah to place of utter brokenness before God, leaving her feeling BARREN and her soul BITTER. Somehow she felt she had missed God's best. Perhaps the grace of God upon her life to bear children had somehow slipped away. However the desire never left but brought her into a place of desperation before God. Little did she know the Lord was setting her up for a major breakthrough!

So many of you even right now have your hearts filled with desires before the Lord. There are just some things that your heart cannot shake. One thing we must remember however is the key to receiving what we desire is to align our hearts with the heart of the Father. When we do that we can be sure that those true desires that enter into our hearts come directly from Him because we have made it our aim to want what He wants and ultimately to desire what He desires. Even so, take heart my beloved brothers and sisters. Just because the fruition of these things does not happen suddenly does not mean it will not happen at all. Could it be that God is setting the stage to work miraculously on your behalf? May it be that the Lord is allowing you to enter a season of desperation so when it does come to pass He gets all the glory? When we delight ourselves in Him, He will give us the desires of our hearts!

As if this weren't enough for Hannah to go through, she had adversaries that looked down on her and even provoked her because of her condition. What was wrong with Hannah? Was there some deficiency in her life or perhaps this was God's way of punishing her for some sin in her life? God forbid! Remember beloved that there will be people who first criticize you for those things you desire, even if those desires truly came from God! They will claim you are reaching for something that is outside of your rightful place. Without saying it, they are really saying you are unworthy and undeserving of such a thing. Of course you are! None of us are deserving of any of God's greatest gifts! All we receive is through the grace found in Jesus Christ. Secondly, there will be people that will judge you for something you don't have that they think you should now possess. But what they don't understand is the timing and seasons of God. He will give us these things in His perfect timing—not in theirs!

I want to encourage you in this very moment not to be discouraged if the desires God has given you have not manifested as of yet. Continue to walk with the Lord, worship Him, serve Him, and delight in Him. Hannah in due season saw the manifestation of God's promise before her very eyes, giving birth to Samuel. And in the days ahead you also will receive the promise of the Father to receive the very desires of your heart.

SAMUEL

TAKEN

DAY 25

And the ark of God was taken; and the two sons of Eli, Hophni and Phinehas, were slain.

—1 Samuel 4:11 KJV

Samuel had been raised up for such a time as this. Serving the Lord even from a young age, Samuel was established as a prophet of the Lord. What a glorious privilege afforded him by God. To represent God to His people was no light thing. As exciting as the call of God was it was also a heavy responsibility not to be taken lightly. Samuel's call into the ministry was timely considering the state of the nation of Israel during that time. Samuel would serve as a powerful prophetic voice during a time of moral decay. And even now God is raising up Samuels to declare the word of the Lord even in the midst of all that is going around us!

It seemed no sooner had Samuel been established by God he immediately was confronted with a multitude of challenges. Eli, the presiding high priest, and his sons were in the process of being ousted by God. Before you know it, the Israelites are engaged in battle with their enemies, the Philistines. To make matters really worse, the ark of God is taken from the people of God. Samuel surely was raised by God during a time of national crisis. The Lord always has His remnant of faithful prophetic voices even in the midst of social and national turmoil. Those who will stand up for righteousness and boldly proclaim the word of the Lord. In the midst of difficulties, don't doubt the call of God on your life but rather allow those challenges to confirm what the Lord is accomplishing in and through you.

The ark of God for the nation of Israel represented God's abiding presence with His people. Think of the devastation brought to both Samuel and the people to see the ark of God carried away and taken by the Philistines. As servants and leaders of the Most High God, what would we ever do without His presence? What would our church services, our times of gathering for prayer and worship, and our times of seeking the Lord be without His manifest presence? It would be utter desperation. It would bring us back to a place of deep hunger and thirst for the presence and glory of God. Could it be that sometimes the Lord will withdraw the enjoyment of His presence in our lives in order to draw us deeper into Him? Yes indeed the Lord will not because He does not love us but because He loves us with an everlasting love and knows what it will take to get us out of our comforts and back to Himself.

Samuel did not have an easy ministry and the same is true for many of you. God has raised *you* up for such a time as this also, but you are immediately faced with the challenges of the culture all around you. And not just in the culture but also within the house of God, there are those who will not make it easy for you to do and be all that God has called you to be. Even Samuel had to endure serving with Eli and his wicked sons for a season. Right now there are some of you who are being tested and being faithful although there are those in the house of God who seem to set up obstacles in your path. Be faithful, for God will deal with everything that is done in His house. In Samuel's day and ministry, there came a point of swift transition as God would deal with Eli and his sons. Even so, God will deal with those who surround you with impure motives and ungodly intentions. It may seem as if nothing is changing and then all of a sudden there is a shift in the atmosphere and the hand of God begins to move and put things in their proper place.

In our lives it can seem at times as if the presence of God is TAKEN but I want to assure you that the Spirit of God has not left you, and He never will. Use those times of dryness and desperation to hunger and thirst for the Lord like never before! Soon the fresh rains of His Spirit will once again saturate your soul!

ELIJAH

STRENGTH FOR THE JOURNEY

DAY 26

*So he got up and ate and drank, and the food gave him enough
strength to travel forty days and forty nights to Mount Sinai, the
mountain of God.*

—1 Kings 19:8 NLT

Elijah had just experienced an amazing victory in the Lord.
Defeating the false prophets of Baal, Elijah proved that there was One
True and Living God who answered by fire! No doubt Elijah was a
mighty man of God, a literal mouthpiece of God for the people and
the leadership during that time. He was bold, courageous, and unwill-
ing to compromise, and his ministry was validated by the power and
presence of God.

But with victory must come vigilance. With every victory comes
attached with it the agenda of the enemy to take out the servants of
God. Elijah experienced this very thing. It wasn't long after God's
mighty hand moved on Mount Carmel that Jezebel threatened the
life of Elijah. He went from mountain high to valley low, and very
quickly. My brothers and sisters, as we advance in the kingdom of
God we must always be ready and on guard against the tactics of the
Enemy. We may seemingly overcome some great obstacle in our lives,
but it will not be long before the attacks come.

Elijah had become a man on the run. Fearing for his life, he
headed straight into the wilderness. One may understand the fear

that must have entered the heart of Elijah along with the stress of the situation. So much so that Elijah literally isolated himself from the world around him. That is the temptation for you and me also. When things get difficult, instead of reaching out to those God has placed around us we may hide away in shame and even in self-pity.

Here we see that God truly uses the weak things of the world to accomplish His mighty purposes in the earth. As powerful as Elijah was in the Lord, how quickly he began to sink emotionally, even to the point of wanting to end his own life! How dangerous it is to be led by our emotions! Only truth is a solid foundation to walk on, not how we feel! When we walk by how we feel we are walking on sinking sand. When we walk according to the Word of God, we are declaring what God has already said! You may even feel like the circumstances of life are too much to bear. You are not sure how much more you can take. But I want to assure you that God will give you the grace to get through it like He did for Elijah. And new STRENGTH will soon be your portion from your God!

My testimony originated in a situation just like Elijah. My life had seemed to tailspin out of control. I wasn't sure how much more I could take. One day I sat on my bed with my head between my knees, wondering if I could go on. In that moment, my dear brothers and sisters, the Spirit of the Lord spoke directly to me and told me in so many words my need for Jesus and how Jesus was a Friend to me. I can't explain it other than it was an encounter with the Living God! My life has never been the same from that point on. Jesus and the power of His Holy Spirit have radically changed and transformed my life.

Elijah had gotten so weak, so tired, so exhausted that he decided to sit under a juniper tree and fall fast asleep. He was at the end of his rope. He had been stripped of all his confidences. He had come to the end of himself. In that moment, God sent one of His angels to minister strength to His tired prophet. Where Elijah ended, God began a new work in Elijah. Where we end, God does the same in us! He will give us strength for the journey!

ELISHA

WHY OF WEEPING

DAY 27

And Hazael said, "Why is my lord weeping?"

—2 Kings 8:12a NKJV

Elisha longed for a double portion of God's Spirit that was upon Elijah and he most certainly received his request. But it wouldn't be long before he realized that operating in the prophetic realm would at times be grieving to his very soul. By the Spirit of God Elisha was given insight to the evil and wickedness King Hazael would perform and carry out. And it brought the prophet Elisha to a place of brokenness and weeping to think of what would soon take place all around him and the nation of Israel.

I truly believe we are living in a time and season where the Lord is raising up a generation of prophetic voices who will stand for righteousness and grieve with all the atrocities going on around them. When a heart is aligned with the heart of the Father, one cannot help but be burdened with that which weighs heavily upon the heart of God. True prophets of God manifest what is on the heart of God to those around them. Even when things get difficult and their word from God is not so encouraging they are faithful to share and declare the word of the Lord.

Even so there are many of you right now who are weeping on the inside due to all that is taking place around you. When you begin to think of the further spiritual and moral decay that is still yet to come tears begin to stream down your face. Some will think it strange the sincere care and concern you have for what is taking place. Even in the church there will be those who cannot understand your fervent desire to see things put in their rightful place. They may even ask, "Why are you weeping?"

The danger is that when the culture changes that the church is forced to lower its standard to what society says is right rather than the authority of the Word of God. Like Elisha, we must be faithful to the word of the Lord and stand firm to what we know is pleasing and acceptable in the sight of God. Elisha was not always popular for proclaiming God's voice to every listening ear. But earning the praise of God is more important than the praise of men. We shall not give account to mankind judgment day but to the One who created, called, and commissioned us into His service. You may feel segregated from others and looked down upon because of your obedience to the Lord, but take heart that when you are disapproved by people you are approved by God. You may anger others by standing up for what is right but you will bless the heart of God as His sons and daughters. You are that prophetic voice paving way for the coming of the Lord!

Even as I write this I am encouraged by the Lord that He keeps an official record of every tear shed by His most precious people. Even in those moments of weeping in solitary silence we often forget the Lord is ever watching and storing up every tear that falls to the ground. I am reminded of the words of the Psalmist in **Psalm 56:8: "You keep track of all my sorrows. You have collected all my tears in your bottle. You have recorded each one in your book"** (NLT). My dearly beloved brothers and sisters, that which is on the forefront of your hearts is also on the forefront of His heart. Every burden, every weight, every care is not only your concern, but His concern. Let us take comfort that the Lord knows our sorrows and that He Himself knows what it is to suffer. Even the Scriptures tell us in **John 11:35, "Jesus wept"** (KJV).

Weeping may endure for a night, but joy cometh in the morning.

—Psalm 30:5b KJV

NEHEMIAH

REBUILDING THE RUINS

DAY 28

But now I said to them, "You know very well what trouble we are in. Jerusalem lies in ruins, and its gates have been destroyed by fire. Let us rebuild the wall of Jerusalem and end this disgrace!"

—Nehemiah 2:17 NLT

Nehemiah certainly was a visionary. Talk about a man with a burden and a passion for God and His people. This man was willing to take extraordinary steps of faith out of what was comfortable to Him in order see Jerusalem and its walls restored and REBUILT once again. There is no doubt this was a devastating scene. King Nebuchadnezzar and the Babylonians had completely wiped Jerusalem out. But with the breaking down there was also the promise of the building up once again of a city whose King was the God of heaven. The same God that promised after seventy years of captivity He would bring His people back into their land and re-establish them once again. This was such a time for the people of God. A time to be BUILT UP!

While God was certainly concerned for the re-establishment of the walls surrounding Jerusalem, God desired so zealously to see His people thriving and their lives abounding in His blessings once again. God's people were at the bottom of the barrel. They had been brought down to nothing. A great stripping down had taken place in their lives. All that was left was the stench of smoldering fire from the ruins that remained. This is where the Lord loves to step in and take that which is broken and make it beautiful!

Even as you read this you may feel that your life is in complete ruins. For a time and season everything was well with you. Life could not have been better. And then just when it seemed that everything was being held together something tragic and unexpected takes place. For some of you an event so debilitating that it has left you broken, hurting, and left to pick up the pieces of what once was. In the ruins of our lives it can be very hard to see any good that could possibly come from our circumstances. Hope is nowhere to be found despite how desperately we seek it. But now is the time to be reminded that our God is in the business of REBUILDING THE RUINS and He will take the ashes of our lives and by His grace revive us once again!

It is encouraging for us to be reminded even in this time and season that the Lord sometimes will allow us to broken down but only so that we may look up to Him for the help only He can provide. Even as the walls surrounding Jerusalem were burned with fire so the Lord will allow His refining fire into our lives to burn away the excess and those things hindering our walk with Him! Every man and woman of God will be touched by the fire of God as it will purify our hearts and lives. Without the fire we are left to our own selfish and carnal ways.

Often and most times unintentionally we carry on with our daily lives and forget how desperate we are for the Lord and His presence. The Lord will then use the current circumstances to remind us and cause us to remember how much we really need Him! If you feel broken down and like you are in the fiery furnace, take heart, for the Lord is the One who controls just how hot things will get! Soon you will come through shining radiantly for the Lord!

What areas of your lives are broken down? Is it in your relationship with someone? Is it within your finances? Is it in the realm of your emotions? Perhaps even in your relationship with Jesus Christ you have allowed your heart to stray from Him. Please receive this encouraging word from the Lord. Now is the time to be built once again. There is no better place for our lives to be built on. None other than upon the Solid Rock of Jesus Christ. The Lord is rebuilding the ruins!

JOB

FRIENDS OR FOES?

DAY 29

Yet my friends laugh at me,
for I call on God and expect an answer.
I am a just and blameless man,
yet they laugh at me.

—Job 12:4 NLT

As if losing his children weren't bad enough. Not to mention all of his wealth. And to top it off a wife who counseled him to curse and renounce God and die. If a man needed comfort in his lifetime this would have been it. When people make poor choices to their own ruin, it is not so surprising to those around them. But Job was a true man of God. Job defined what a true worshiper should be at heart. He worshiped God for who He was and not for what He could give to him. Even when all was lost including his own health, Job boldly declared, ***"The Lord gave, and the Lord has taken away; blessed be the name of the Lord" (Job 1:21b NKJV).***

But just when it couldn't have gotten any worse, along come three of Job's closest companions. If any should've shown sympathy to Job it was these men. Isn't it interesting how the circumstances you face will reveal who your true friends really are? In a time when Job's friend should have come alongside of him with support and understanding, they were too busy trying to pinpoint just what Job had done to deserve all of this suffering. In doing so they concocted multiple false conclusions including accusing him of falling into sin thereby bringing the judgment of God upon Himself. But they were tragically wrong in their estimation! Aren't you glad we have a friend who sticks closer than a brother? Even when our earthly friends fail us, there is a Friend we have found in God Himself who will never fail us. You are a FRIEND of God!

Even some of you have gone and are going through this very thing. During the most difficult seasons of your lives when you needed friendship the most, you found it the least in your supposed friends. Even some of the friends that did stick by you were occupied with reasoning your suffering out rather than just being a source of comfort and encouragement. Not every person the Lord allows into our lives will fit into this category. But few and far between are those loyal and faithful friends given to us by God!

The question for you and me is: what kind of friend are we to those around us? Are we more of a friend or foe to those people the Lord has placed in our lives? Over the years I have lost many, many friends. Sometimes it was due to transitions in our lives. Other times it was due to the choices and decisions made by my friends. And there are many occurrences when it was due to poor choices on my part. Many of you reading this know exactly what I'm talking about and have been there yourselves! The Lord desires for us to be those caliber of friends that replicate the kind of friend God is to us. He listens to us in our pain. He is faithful to us though we fail. He is not inconsistent but is rather unwavering in His love towards us. What a model of friendship the Lord has displayed for us!

One of the most difficult trials of our lives is when we walk in the call of God for our lives and yet our so-called friends laugh at us. My dear brothers and sisters, I want to encourage you with this word from the Lord. When the Lord begins to promote and raise you up, it is often those closest to you that will resist and even oppose what the Spirit of God is doing in your lives. Shouldn't it be the very opposite? No wonder Jesus said in **Matthew 13:57b,** "A *prophet is honored everywhere except in his own hometown and among his own family"* (NLT). Your friends may act like foes, but keep pressing forward despite the opinions of others. There is one ultimate Friend we were made to please and that is the Friend we have found in God.

DAVID

LET THE DAVIDS ARISE

DAY 30

*Then Samuel asked, "Are these all the sons you have?" "There is still
the youngest," Jesse replied. "But he's out in the fields watching the
sheep and goats." "Send for him at once," Samuel said. "We will not
sit down to eat until he arrives." . . . So as David stood there among
his brothers, Samuel took the flask of olive oil he had brought and
anointed David with the oil. And the Spirit of the LORD came powerfully upon David from that day on. Then Samuel returned to Ramah.*

—1 Samuel 16:11, 13 NLT

The time had come for a new king. With position comes promotion,
which comes only from the Lord. Little did David know it—God had
been preparing him in the fields and in the wilderness for a plan far
greater than he could have ever imagined. It would not be easy, but
David's destiny was beginning to unfold before his very eyes. What
some would consider nothing more than a ruddy and rugged youth,
God saw as a mighty warrior and man of God who would rise to
kingship. Oh, to see others the way God sees them! Then maybe, just
maybe we would begin to see the God potential in others! Seeing
others not just the way they are presently, but seeing all that they can
become through the mighty power of God and the Spirit of God at
work within them. Aren't you so glad that God sees you from end to
beginning all that you will become for His glory!

I can only imagine in the natural there would have been many reasons to put any other man besides David into the kingship after Saul. But it wasn't natural, human abilities that God was looking for. Nor was the Lord impressed with the outward cosmetic features of a man. What moved the heart and hand of God was what was found on the inside of the man. With God the inward parts are always preferred to the outward. David was such a man who was inwardly devoted to the Lord.

Whether anyone else realized it or not David was already destined to be king. God had chosen His man and no one could take that from him! Not even the gates of hell can stop the hand of God once He has made His decision. My brothers and sisters, no one can take from you the place, position, and purpose for which you were created! There is only one of you! Rise up and take your place in the kingdom of God!

I wonder how David must have felt. Jesse was willing to place every one of his sons before the prophet Samuel. All of them that is, except David! Can you imagine having your own father not even believe in you? Did he have any confidence in his youngest son, David? How hurtful, embarrassing, and shameful this must have been for David. Even so the voice of God came to Samuel and instructed him clearly to bring David and anoint him to be the next king. Despite even what Jesse had assumed about his own son, God would raise David up farther than any of the human limitations placed upon him.

There are some of you reading this who understand well the pain of having others not believe or support the call of God upon your life. Isn't it true that some of those closest to you fit this description? Please allow me to speak prophetically over you. When God raises you up to the call upon your life, those same people will bask in awe at the work and power of God in your life. They will think back to who you were and marvel at what you've become in the Lord. And God will get all the glory, for only He could perform this in your lives!

In some ways I can identify with some of the hardships David experienced. My father was never around and in no way a support for me. I had no example to follow. No man I could call "Dad" and seek counsel from. Years later when I had an encounter with the Spirit of God, He led me to faith in Jesus Christ and I started to learn that I had a Father in heaven who loved me and called me as His own. Presently as I look back, I see His hand upon my life raising me up just as He did with David. While everyone else may have discredited me and the ministry the Lord called me to, God Himself would continue to envelop my life with His presence and open doors that no one could shut and bring me into realms of ministry that would bring glory to His name! And He is still doing that work in my life, raising me up to all that He has called me to be.

I desire to speak into your lives even now that God is raising you up just like He did with David! Others may attempt to disqualify you. Man may count you out and try to place you on the shelf. But people are not in charge of your destiny! God will fulfill His plans and purposes through those individuals who are surrendered to Him! Many of you right now are in the fields of God's preparation. You are tending to the sheep. You are doing the difficult work in private. Many times it may seem that what you are doing is not making an impact or has no lasting value. But I am here to tell you now that you are in the place of preparation to walk into your God-given purpose. Stay faithful and obedient for soon God is going to raise you up higher than you could imagine! IT IS TIME FOR THE DAVIDS TO ARISE!

DAVID

ESCAPE TO ENGEDI

DAY 31

So Saul quit chasing David and returned to fight the Philistines. Ever since that time, the place where David was camped has been called the Rock of Escape. Then David went up from there and dwelt in strongholds at En-gedi.

—1 Samuel 23:28-29 NLT

What a wonderful place that rock of escape must have been for David and his men. Especially for David seeing there was a bounty out for his life. But while running from death, David found life on that rock as God deterred Saul's evil schemes from coming to pass. Oh, the life we've found on the Rock of Jesus Christ! We at one time were literally walking in death but now we have been made alive in Jesus Christ, filled with His Holy Spirit and given new life! The Enemy had a plan to take us out and keep us blinded from the truth of the gospel. But neither death nor the Devil could hold us down for they were both defeated at the cross of Jesus Christ. Hallelujah!

All of us need a place of escape, don't we? Each of us have our Sauls that are chasing us down, those trials that constantly seem to be on our tails. We understand what it means to have pressure and stress on every side. Aren't you thankful our God is a place of refuge and strength for His people?! Isn't it wonderful that the Lord is a place of safety for His sons and daughters? **Proverbs 18:10 tells us, "The name of the LORD is a strong tower; the righteous run to it and are** *safe"* (NKJV). The Lord provides a covering of shade from the heat of the sun. The Lord provides shelter from the winds and rain. In the turmoil of life *He* is our only escape and place of refuge. People of God, let us run into Him!

Not only did David find that rock of escape, but He went a bit further into a place called Engedi. Engedi is an oasis found just west of the Dead Sea. Filled with caves and streams of flowing water, this oasis provides a source of refreshment and nourishment in the midst of desert-like conditions. The word Engedi literally means "fountain of the kid." It was in this isolated place that David would drink from the fountains of God's living water. It was in this place of ESCAPE that he would find refreshment and nourishment for his soul from the Living God. In the midst of our trials and trouble one of the best things we can do is find that Engedi in our lives, that place of escape where we can receive from and be ministered to by the Lord. The Lord is calling His people back to the secret place, and back to that place of escape that we might have a glorious encounter with Him!

Right now you may feel just like David. You've been running, running, running and now it's time to sit and soak in the presence of God in that place of escape. The Enemy loves to see the people of God busy. If he can keep us busy enough not to spend quality time in the presence of God he will make every attempt to do so. If we are prayerless, we will be powerless. If we are without His Word in us we will be weak. If we fail to spend time in the presence of God, we will be fresh prey for the Enemy and for the battles that are continually all around us. Perhaps you are reading this right now and you sense the tug of the Holy Spirit to get back into that solitary place with the Lord. The Lord is calling you to your personal Engedi!

As overwhelming as life can be, this is a call back to where we should have been all along. Sometimes we just have to make that decision to stop what we are doing and run to the Savior. Are our lives filled with stuff or are we rich in the things of the Spirit? Are we constantly running or have we learned to know when to retreat to that place of escape? Truth be told, everything that we need is found at the feet of the One who gave His all for us. The question is: How will we respond to His invitation? Now is the time to ESCAPE TO ENGEDI!

DAVID

HOW LONG?

DAY 32

How long must I struggle with anguish in my soul,
with sorrow in my heart every day?
How long will my enemy have the upper hand?

—Psalm 13:2 NLT

Psalm 13 is a psalm of transition. David begins in utter despair, but in a handful of verses his sorrow is turned into rejoicing and joy unspeakable. How can that be? How does a man so discouraged become so encouraged in such a seemingly short amount of time? How can a man in so much pain offer in the same conversation such praises to the God of heaven?

The answer to this question is David had a real relationship with the Lord. He didn't understand the reason for everything he had to endure. There were many unknowns in the life of David, but what was known of David is the faithfulness of his God! Even in the barrenness and emptiness of his soul David encouraged himself in the Lord and reminded himself of the very character of his God.

There were many times David felt so alone, so desolate, even forsaken and yet he had to look past his feelings and rely upon his faith in the Living God. If David had relied solely on how he felt he may well have stayed in his lowly spiritual state. But because David was a man of faith, he knew where to place his trust and confidence—in the Lord! David was still a man after God's own heart. David was still beloved in the eyes of God. And so are you, my dear brothers and sisters! Do not gauge the love of God for you based on your circumstances and or how you feel. Your God will come through! A transition is coming! Sorrow turned to joy is yours! This too shall pass!

Many of you right now can empathize with David. You have dedicated your lives to the Lord Jesus Christ, yet you feel dry and desperate for the presence of God once again. Let me share something with you to encourage you to the depths of your soul. If you didn't recognize your need and necessity for the Spirit of God like the air you breathe, then there would be cause to worry! But you know your God! You desire His presence! You hunger and thirst for Him! Soon and very soon you will once experience the blessedness of His nearness in your lives!

We have to admire the transparency of King David as He writes under the influence of the Spirit of God. We have to respect his honesty and sincerity as he communicates the condition of his soul and his deep desire for the Lord. Although anointed as king he was not entitled to a life or calling without its valleys of despair. In fact, God was using all of these experiences to further shape and mature him to be fit as a king not only in the earthly realm but as a king in the kingdom of God. If you desire to be used by God mightily, then these types of trials will also be yours. But the end result is usefulness in the kingdom of God! We often look at ministries that are powerfully used of God but seldom look at the price that was paid to achieve the spiritual success they have attained.

My brothers and sisters, I can tell you that I myself have been through many dry and desert places, but God has brought me out rich every single time! Though the waiting may seem long, the reward of waiting will most surely pay its dividends! Soon the garments of praise will replace the spirit of heaviness and the oil of joy for your mourning (Isaiah 61:3). No matter HOW LONG it may seem, your God will come through and restore to you the rejoicing of your hearts.

DAVID

BLESSED

Blessed is he whose transgression is forgiven,
Whose sin is covered.

—Psalm 32:1 NKJV

Who has not felt the sting of failure? Which one of us has not experienced the sadness when faced with our own shortcomings? David surely had and he knew it well. Although David was considered a man after God's own heart, that did not decrease the danger of falling into temptation. Not only did David give into the desires of his own fleshly passion, but He killed in order to get what he wanted. While King David should have been out to battle leading his army, he decided to stay back and settled into a place of complacency. It wasn't long until David found himself gazing upon and going after another man's wife. David longed for Bathsheba and murdered her husband, Uriah, to get what he wanted. But sin has its price and for a year's time David would walk in a season of deep grieving because of the sin of his soul. How could that happen? How could a man so in love with the Lord commit such a thing? How could such a man so anointed by God do this very thing?

How many of you know that those God uses most powerfully are not those who are so-called perfect! God delights in using those who are imperfect and have a heart tender towards Him! We are just the imperfect called and chosen by a perfect God. There was only one perfect man and that was the God-Man Jesus Christ! But as Paul writes in **1 Corinthians 1:26,** *"For you see your calling, brethren, that not many wise according to the flesh, not many mighty, not many noble,* **ARE CALLED"** (NKJV, emphasis mine). Those who recognize their wretched state before a holy God are often those God calls and raises up and uses mightily for His purposes!

Right now as you read this, you may be discouraged by some sudden failure in your lives. You may have completely blown it. Those words you said that you can never take back. The sudden loss of your temper. Those compromises of the flesh you gave into. Perhaps you lost your patience with your spouse or children. Take heart, my beloved brothers and sisters! You certainly are not alone in your struggle! Oh, it may seem like you are the only one in the whole world who is battling and contending for victory in some area. And the Enemy loves to have you feel that way. He wants you to feel like you are segregated in your struggle in order that he might accuse you and bring a sense of condemnation upon your soul. It is then we must get back up and keep walking and working on those areas of our lives with the help and power of the Holy Spirit. The Enemy may condemn, but it is the Spirit of God that convicts and draws us back to Himself. It is not those who fall down that are considered complete failures. It is those who refuse to get up, and try once again. As Thomas Edison said, *"The most certain way to succeed is always to try just one more time."*

David considered himself a blessed man. The word blessed here literally means happy. But what was it that made him so? Was it the day that Samuel poured the horn of oil over his head to distinguish him as God's chosen and anointed one? Perhaps it was the mighty victory the Lord gave him over the giant Philistine, Goliath! Or how about the multitude of mighty deliverances God provided for David out of the hand of his enemies? Surely all of these things would cause the heart of David to be blessed and happy.

But I suppose one of the greatest reliefs for David was the day God put away his sin. Despite the greatness of David's sin God's grace was greater! Some of you reading this right now need to be reminded that the Lord has *put away* your sin as well! Moreover, God went as far as to say in **Hebrews 10:17,** *"And their sins and iniquities will I remember no more"* (KJV). Oh, if not for the cross of Jesus Christ! He has washed away my stains! He has taken all my shame! There is forgiveness in His name! I don't care how bad you've failed. It doesn't matter how far you have strayed from the Lord. This day the Lord calls you back and calls you blessed! Oh, how happy and blessed are those who have God's forgiveness imparted to them!

ISAIAH

I SAW THE LORD

DAY 34

In the year that King Uzziah died, I saw the Lord sitting on a throne,
high and lifted up, and the train of His robe filled the temple. . . . So I
said: "Woe is me, for I am undone because I am a man of unclean lips,
And I dwell in the midst of a people of unclean lips;
For my eyes have seen the King,
The Lord of hosts."

—Isaiah 6:1, 5 NKJV

While one man had experienced death, another man was receiving an incredible vision of the very throne room of God! As God would commission Isaiah as a prophet to the nations, his encounter with the Living God would change the course and direction of his life. Truly, Isaiah would never be the same! For what is man in comparison with the glory and splendor of God? Which one of us could stand before the Lord in our own righteousness or because of something good we have done? There is not one of us that is not in need of the glorious grace and forgiveness of God found only in the cross of Jesus Christ.

The prophet Isaiah found this out very quickly. It's very interesting to hear all that people will say in the presence of God as they stand before Him. But scripturally whenever a true encounter with the Lord took place, there was always such a sense of awe and wonder that the individual immediately recognized their unworthiness before God. Isaiah SAW the Lord and instantly was confronted with who he really was in the sight of the Lord. Amazingly enough, God chooses to use broken vessels just like Isaiah who although not perfect are willing to admit their own iniquity and humble themselves before a holy God.

This should bring great encouragement to our hearts. How often we have been used mightily of God and yet fail so much. One moment we are full of the Spirit of God, operating in His gifts and ministering before the Lord. And the next we are saying something we shouldn't, looking at something we shouldn't, or doing something we shouldn't. Yet God has still called us, chosen us, and included us in His great plans and purposes! Isaiah immediately recognized his failings as a man, and God cleansed Isaiah and sent him out in the strength of His Spirit to accomplish what he could not do in his own strength.

Today you may be walking around with weighty bags of guilt and shame on your shoulders. Perhaps you are wondering how God could ever use someone like you with all of your sin and failures. But let me remind you beloved that the Lord did not choose you or set His love upon you because of your own worthiness. He has ordained you because He is good and because of His great grace towards you. No longer do you have to carry the weight of your shame, because Jesus dealt with it once and for all on the cross!

As servants of the Most High God, what we really need is a greater glimpse of God! We need to encounter Him like never before. We must be desperate for the presence of God! The more we are with the Lord the more we understand that without Him we are nothing. As Charles Spurgeon once said, *"The best man is man at best."* How true is that statement! We must always remember it is His mighty power at work within us that enables to accomplish our God-given purpose. Isaiah SAW the Lord and the more we see Him the more we will desire Him.

JEREMIAH

I WILL REFRESH THE WEARY

DAY 35

"I will refresh the weary and satisfy the faint."

—Jeremiah 31:25 NIV

What a word fitly spoken by the Lord over His people. He knew the pain they had endured. He knew well the sorrows of their hearts. He saw every tear that fell from their eyes. The Lord was now reminding His people of His great love for them and His promise of restoration to not only their lands and possessions but to their souls, which desperately needed a touch from God.

Isn't it interesting that one could possess all the money in the world and yet still be empty in one's soul? One could have the largest house, the nicest car, all the accessories one could wish for and yet still have an aching for more in one's heart. God's people had attempted to fill their hearts with various idols only to find emptiness and vanity. God allowed them to experience the pain that accompanied their choices, but He was also bringing them to a place of revival, renewal, and restoration. One touch from God would prove to change the whole course of their lives. When we experience His touch in our lives, it will drastically change us from the inside out.

Perhaps even now God is drawing you to a place of REFRESHMENT in His presence. Did you realize there is a climate and atmosphere that the Lord desires you to live in? It is within the atmosphere of His presence where we find all that we truly need! The presence of God will mend our broken hearts. God's presence will bring joy where there was sorrow. The Living Water of God's Spirit will pour life and sustenance where there was a vacuum of emptiness God created us and intended for us to dwell in His powerful presence. Until we learn to get back to that place, we will become weary through the process of trying to replace the Lord with futile things that will not satisfy.

Even so the daily grind of life can cause us to nearly faint. Things can change so suddenly in our lives and without warning. There you are working day in and day out. You are doing the best you can to live for the Lord and provide for your family and then it happens. It could be that unexpected doctor's report. Perhaps it's that person you trusted and confided in that betrayed you. The pile of mounting bills that never seems to go away. Any one of these things can leave us feeling tired and faint. The exhaustion that stress brings can be indescribable. But praise the God of heaven there is a remedy for the weary soul.

My beloved brothers and sisters, I want to remind you that there is a well that never runs dry. When you are in this place of weariness, just as I have been many times, there is a place of spiritual refreshment that is found only in the presence of God. Even Jesus during His earthly ministry would take times to rest because He Himself had become weary at times. Could it be now God is calling you into a time of rest and refreshment in His presence? Do you sense the Lord drawing you to turn off the distractions and to get before Him? Often I wonder how much of God's blessings we miss simply because we have failed to come before His presence. Now is a great time as any to reprioritize our time and get alone with God. We have His wonderful promise that as we do, He WILL REFRESH THE WEARY and satisfy the longings of our hearts.

I want you to imagine with me a river so wide and so enlarged that it has overflowed its banks and saturated the surrounding land. I truly believe the Lord desires to satisfy our souls in such a way that we are filled to overflowing with the presence of the Living God. Once the floodgates of heaven open over our lives, there is no stopping the flow of His precious Spirit. This is a word for each of you my beloved brothers and sisters. Soon the weariness you are now experiencing will be replaced with the supernatural strength of God's Spirit. He will refresh the weary!

HEALTH AND HEALING

DAY 36

"I will give you back your health and heal your wounds," says the LORD.

—Jeremiah 30:17a NLT

What a promise from God to bring *health and healing* to His people. Truly He is Jehovah Rophe, the Lord our healer! It wasn't just their physical bodies that needed God's healing touch. The emotional and spiritual state of God's people had also deteriorated down to nothing. Given they had lost everything, their mental state at this point was anything but encouraging. When the world chews us up and spits us out there is no guarantee of a remedy for our hurting souls. But when the Lord allows us as His people to receive wounds, He always does so with the purpose of eventually mending and healing our broken hearts. Praise the Lord He does not keep us in our crippled condition! Oh, the wonderful grace of God towards His people! ***"Come, let us return to the LORD. He has torn us to pieces; now he will HEAL us. He has injured us; now he will bandage our wounds" (Hosea 6:1 NLT, emphasis mine).***

There are some of you reading this that have been patiently waiting upon the Lord for a miraculous physical healing. It may be a heart issue, a kidney problem, or a blood disorder of some type. Whate'er the ailment may be, it is not above God to send His healing power! Once the Lord determines to heal an individual, the sickness that binds you will be eradicated and removed from your physical body.

When God speaks, every chain is broken, including those infirmities that hold us captive. Even for those of you reading this right now may the healing power of God touch you right where you are!

Just because God has not answered our prayers for healing immediately does not mean that God will not heal us! Rather, we are to keep asking, keep seeking, keep knocking until that door opens unto us. God rewards the diligent seeker and those who refuse to give up until they receive a response from heaven. God will honor not only a trusting faith but a persevering faith. Once you have prayed for healing, pray yet again. It might just be when we are willing to believe God even when all previous prayers seem unanswered that the Lord will then send forth the healing we so desire. Pray and believe! Believe while you pray! By His stripes we are healed!

Perhaps you are daring to trust God to heal a dear loved one. It could be your spouse, one of your children, a parent, or a close friend. Watching those you love suffer so much can be one of life's greatest trials. How often we have wished it upon ourselves rather than upon those near to us. Day after day, month after month, even year after year, pain grips our hearts as we watch those we love suffer. How often we have been crying on the inside, desperate to see our situation change for the better.

I want to remind you today of the healing power of God. He can heal our emotions. When I first came to Jesus Christ one of the first things the Lord did was deliver me from depression and anxiety. He can heal the broken pieces of our past. He can mend our hearts and bring us a true joy and peace that passes all understanding. And He can most certainly touch our physical bodies.

We may not always understand the reason for our suffering and why sickness is not always immediately healed by the Lord. But we must persevere and keep praying, keep believing, and keep hoping in the Lord.

EZEKIEL

BREATH OF GOD

DAY 37

He led me all around among the bones that covered the valley floor. They were scattered everywhere across the ground and were completely dried out. Then he asked me, "Son of man, can these bones become living people again?" "O Sovereign LORD," I replied, "you alone know the answer to that." Then he said to me, "Speak a prophetic message to these bones and say, 'Dry bones, listen to the word of the LORD! This is what the Sovereign LORD says: Look! I am going to put breath into you and make you live again!'"

—Ezekiel 37:2-5 NLT

Ezekiel, along with his contemporary Jeremiah, had one of the most difficult ministries afforded him by God. Anointed by the Spirit of God as both priest and prophet, Ezekiel was sent to the people of God who were held captive in Babylon under the wicked reign of King Nebuchadnezzar. Ezekiel's ministry consisted of communicating difficult truth to a people who were dull of hearing. Does this sound familiar? Has the work of the ministry become difficult? Does it seem that those you have been sent to do not listen with ears to hear? Take heart, my brothers and sisters. Ezekiel's life and ministry will encourage your hearts then.

Ezekiel's ministry was also earmarked with the supernatural workings of God's Spirit. Ezekiel was privileged by God to receive some astounding visions, including those of the very throne room of God! Holy, Holy, Holy, Lord God Almighty! The One Who was and is and is to come! Such insight was given him by God, but also to serve as a great encouragement to the prophet as he proclaimed the word of the Lord. With the mayhems of ministry God also supplies His provision of grace in proportion to the hardships that lie ahead. You may be experiencing the harsh realities of serving the Lord and His people presently, but know that God will sustain you through it all. Stay faithful and obedient and the abundant blessings of God will follow.

Within the visions of God, the Lord shows Ezekiel a valley filled with dry bones. Not only did a good portion of the nation of Israel die physically but they had died spiritually and moral decay had set in. Herein we see the faithfulness of God to His people. They had been idolatrous and adulterous towards the Lord. They had chosen their own ways over God's ways. Now they were facing the consequences of their choices but God still had a plan for them. Sometimes the Lord will allow things to die so that He might resurrect them once again. God was not through with His people and He is not done with you either! He will finish what He's started! He will perfect all that concerns you! He is watching over His word to perform it in your life. Spiritually things may be dry and seemingly dead right now but soon and very soon the breath of God will overtake you and new strength will come by the Spirit of God.

Prophetically we know in context God was speaking directly over the nation of Israel. Although they had disintegrated as a nation, God fulfilled His word by resurrecting them once again as a nation in 1948. But how does this word apply to you and me presently? Please allow me to share this encouraging word from the Lord with you. There are areas of our lives that can be just like this valley: filled with dry bones. It could be your marriage, your relationship with your children, your ministry, your place of employment—even your walk with the Lord. As we submit these areas of our lives to the Lord, He will once again breathe on us and bring to life that which was dead! Don't lose heart, my beloved brothers and sisters. Do not lose sight of the hope found in Jesus Christ. The way things are currently is not the way things will always be! It just might be the Lord is desiring to bring you to the end of yourself so that He can intervene on your behalf. When we truly realize that we are nothing apart from Him, God will take that barren desert of our souls and make it a fruitful garden habituated by His Spirit. Let your prayer today be: ***"Breath of God, breathe on me!"***

CARRIED TO THE COURTS

DAY 38

In the third year of the reign of Jehoiakim king of Judah,
Nebuchadnezzar king of Babylon came to Jerusalem and besieged it.
And the Lord gave Jehoiakim king of Judah into his hand, with some
of the articles of the house of God, which he carried into the land of
Shinar to the house of his god; and he brought the articles into the
treasure house of his god. Then the king instructed Ashpenaz, the
master of his eunuchs, to bring some of the children of Israel and
some of the king's descendants and some of the nobles, young men in
whom there was no blemish, but good-looking, gifted in all wisdom,
possessing knowledge and quick to understand, who had ability to
serve in the king's palace, and whom they might teach the language
and literature of the Chaldeans.

—Daniel 1:1-4 NKJV

Daniel and his three friends had been carried into captivity into the courts of King Nebuchadnezzar. Everything that was familiar to them had been left behind. They were stripped of what was normal to them and brought to a foreign land to serve a king who cared nothing for the God of heaven. It wasn't their fault or their own doings that caused this sudden transition, yet they would be thrusted into the courts of Babylon to bring glory to the Lord. What would unfold in their lives in the days ahead would exceed any expectation they could imagine in their natural minds. Not only did trials and trouble await them, but also through their testing would come the PROMOTION that comes only from God.

Some of you reading this have also experienced the carrying away into circumstances that you could not have foreseen. Life was going as it was and then suddenly a situation arises and it seems you are carried away captive. Now your hearts are gripped with the pain of what once was. Everything has changed and transition is difficult. You didn't ask for this to happen. Perhaps you are suffering at the hand of someone else's poor decision. But here you are, carried to the courts of circumstance. My dear brothers and sisters, if this is you, take heart and know that God is paving the way for not only your testing but your promotion.

It was neither Daniel's nor his three friends' rebellion or disobedience to the Lord that brought them to this place. These men loved the Lord and were committed to serving Him even if it cost their own lives! It was the nation of Israel as a whole that had turned from God and brought the judgment of God upon themselves. But notice that not once do we read of their complaints nor did they point their fingers at God and demand an answer or remedy for what they were going through. Rather, they used the difficulties as a platform to bring glory to the God of heaven. Their interest was not in promoting themselves but in using every opportunity to lift high the name of the Lord.

What an example and lesson laid out before us. Some of you even right now are in the most difficult situations of your lives. But I want to encourage you in this moment that the Lord is going to use the pain you are experiencing to give you an opportunity to bring glory to His name. An untested faith, my brothers and sisters, remains shallow and on the surface, with little depth. But when we are tested and able to *praise God* still even while we ourselves do not understand why we have been carried away, this is most pleasing to the Lord. First Peter 2:20 reminds us, ***"For what credit is it if, when you are beaten for your*** *faults, you take it patiently? But when you do good and suffer, if you take it patiently, this is commendable before God"* (NKJV).

When we do everything we know to be right and still suffer, this can be one of the trying tests of the heart. But I want to remind you of the suffering our precious Lord and Savior, Jesus Christ, went through and endured on our behalf. He was completely innocent yet He was beaten, mocked, scourged, whipped, spit upon, and nailed to the cross. Did you remember that Christ was sinless, absolutely and completely? But He was will to take the suffering patiently in order to redeem and win us back to Himself!

My brothers and sisters despite your difficulty as you patiently wait upon the Lord, He is going to slowly but surely exalt you for His purposes in the kingdom of God. When we humble ourselves as servants just like Daniel and his three friends, we are setting ourselves up so God can use us powerfully! Daniel would eventually rise to the third highest position in Babylon. His three friends were also promoted and placed in positions of prominence. But first, they were tested, tried, and found true! Take heart, my dear friends. Though you are carried to the courts, God is preparing to promote you and usher you to walk in your divine destiny.

HABAKKUK

WAIT FOR IT

DAY 39

"This vision is for a future time.
It describes the end, and it will be fulfilled.
If it seems slow in coming, wait patiently,
for it will surely take place.
It will not be delayed."

—Habakkuk 2:3 NLT

What is it about waiting that makes it so difficult in the natural? More often than not, our flesh screams out for what it wants until it finally receives what it so longs for. When God gives a vision to a man or woman, He does so with the intention that we will patiently wait for the fulfillment of what He has revealed to us. The difficulty lies in our ability to wait upon the Lord to bring about the vision in His timing and in His way! Trying to fulfill God's vision in the scope of our own strength is a prescription for failure. But as we allow the Lord to move and work by His Spirit there is a God-ease and a Sabbath rest we can work from knowing that He who birthed the vision will see it through to completion.

Habakkuk not only had a vision from God but he was desperate to see a change from the current atrocities all around him. Everywhere he turned wickedness seemed to prevail without the divine intervention of God. Does this sound to you anything like our current culture? But Habakkuk would come to learn that God is always working even in the background of our lives to bring about His purposes. Just because we may not see His hand immediately does not mean the Lord isn't busy making preparations for our deliverance. Although it may seem for a season that heaven is silent, it does not mean God is not speaking. We will hear His voice once again. It is the sovereignty of God to do what He wants when He is ready to do it. Your waiting will not bring about disappointment but rather a delight as you witness firsthand the faithfulness of God to do what He said He would do. One word from the Lord will move all of heaven and earth to see His Word accomplished as He so desires.

People of vision are people of passion. They are focused, knowing the direction in which they are moving. They are determined and not willing to give up easily. Individuals with a vision from God are bold and seem to have a spiritual iron within their souls to persevere through the storms of life where others are more prone to retreat from moving forward. My dear brothers and sisters, the Lord knows well the burden and vision that are on your hearts. He is the one who placed that vision in your spirits. He is the one who gave you that revelatory image of what He wants to accomplish. But the Lord never said that it would be an easy smooth road to seeing that vision become a reality. Truth be told it will be quite the opposite! There will be challenges. There will be sudden roadblocks. There will most definitely be opposition to a true vision from God. Take the difficulties you are facing as a confirmation from the Lord that your vision truly is from Him! Always remember that anything worthwhile for the kingdom of God will come at a price. Jesus Christ paid the ultimate price, but each servant, each man or woman of God, will pay a personal price to see the vision come to fruition. Hang in there and be willing to pay the price!

We can learn so much from the prophet Habakkuk as he learns to wait upon the Lord. In the end of his writings, he makes a bold determination to rejoice while he is waiting upon God. **Habakkuk 3:17-18 says, "*Even though the fig trees have no blossoms, and there*** *are no grapes on the vines; even though the olive crop fails, and the fields lie empty and barren; even though the flocks die in the fields, and the cattle barns are empty, yet I will rejoice in the Lᴏʀᴅ! I will be joyful in the God of my salvation!"* (NLT). Let's worship Him in the waiting. As we wait for it, we can be sure that our God is watching over His word to perform it. He who gave the vision will seal it, confirm it, and do it.

MALACHI

BURNING AWAY

DAY 40

He will sit as a refiner and a purifier of silver;
He will purify the sons of Levi,
And purge them as gold and silver,
That they may offer to the LORD
An offering in righteousness.

—Malachi 3:3 NKJV

Show me a man or woman mightily used of God, and I can guarantee they have been touched by the refining fire of God. Many proclaim they so desire to be used powerfully by the Lord, but few consider the cost to what they are asking. But God, my dear brothers and sisters, is in the business of transforming and shaping His servants to make us fit for usefulness in the kingdom of God. Here God was concerned in making sure His priests were holy and pure in both life and service. But how does that happen?

I'm sure if you and I had our own way we would surely choose the easy way. We have this idea that we will reach our full potential while we continue to live in our comforts and what is manageable for our own flesh. But the Lord is calling us to His higher way! Our development as servants of the Most High God will not come on the couch of comfort but rather in His furnace of fire. **First Peter 4:12 reminds us, "Dear friends, don't be surprised at the fiery trials you are going through, as if something strange were happening to you"** (NLT).

Oftentimes unintentionally on our part, we think that we are further along than we really are. But the Lord sees the depths of our hearts and knows what is really on the inside of us. He loves us too much too keep us the same! When the fire of God touches our lives it does a PURIFYING WORK, separating the clean from the unclean. His fire will bring to the surface that which has lain dormant, buried within our hearts. When it manifests itself, God can then purge those things that are unpleasing to Him.

Could it be that what you are facing currently is because the Lord desires to do a much deeper work in you fashioning you into His image? Perhaps the Lord desires to see more of His reflection in you! Are there things in your hearts that God has been speaking to you about that He would like to deal with? Could it be you are holding unforgiveness towards a friend or family member? Is it some attitude you have harbored that He would like to change and bring into alignment with His character? Let us praise Him right now as He is bringing us from glory to glory. We may be a people forged in the fire but more and more we are becoming like Him!

The more of His fire that touches us, the more our offerings of service to God will be marked by purity. All hidden motives and agendas will be exposed in the fire. The more fire we experience, the purer our motives to bring Him glory will be. The fire will strip us of ourselves and fill us with more of Him! More of Him and less of me! Let that be our prayer and desire even in this moment.

My dear brothers and sisters, I want to remind and encourage you that you are priests of the Most High God! The Lord has called you to minister before Him and there is no greater calling or purpose than to walk before the Lord doing what He has called you to do. The more we are committed to His service and kingdom we will understand the purpose of going through the fire. Remember, with great usefulness there is also a great burning away that we will experience.

No matter the wilderness, beloved, I want to encourage you that the Lord not only has gone before you but He will walk with you through it all. This is a word for you, the weary, that through the wilderness, the desert, the fire, the storm, the winds, and the rain, forever He is faithful. He never changes; He always stays the same.

For more information about
Kevin Stevens
&
A Word for the Weary
please visit:

www.kevinstevens.me
kevinstevensministries@gmail.com
@Kevin_A_Stevens
www.facebook.com/authorkevinstevens

For more information about
AMBASSADOR INTERNATIONAL
please visit:

www.ambassador-international.com
@AmbassadorIntl
www.facebook.com/AmbassadorIntl